PONTIAC FIREBIRD

Body, Trim and Glass 1967-1981
Interchangeable Parts Guide

First Published in 2003 by PAH Publishing International
711 Hillcrest, Monett, Missouri 65708 USA
© John R. Miller, 2003, 2021

All rights reserved. With the exception of quoting brief passages for the purposes of review no part of this publication may be reproduced without prior written permission from the Publisher. The information in this book is true and complete to the best of our knowledge. All recommendations are made without any guarantee on part of the author or Publisher, who also disclaim any liability incurred in connection with the use of this data or specific details. Always use jack stands and exercise caution when working on your automobile.

PAH Publishing books are also available at bulk discount for industrial or sale promotional use. Write to Trade Desk-Wholesale Department at the Publisher's address.

We recognize that some words, model names and designations, for example, mentioned herein are the property of the trademark holder. We use them for identification purposes only. This is not an official GM publication.

Used Parts Buyers Guide Firebird Body Trim and Glass, 1967-1981
John R. Miller

p. cm.
Includes index
ISBN: 9780971645943
1. Pontiac Cars-Used Parts 2 Firebird Used Parts. Title 2004, 2021

Cover: 1977 Blue 'Screaming Chicken decal' with nameplates
Back: 1973 Formula Firebird with 455 S.D. top photos 1968 Firebird, 1981 Firebird PMD photos

ACKNOWLEDGMENTS

This book would not have been possible if it were not for the assistance of the individuals. All those individuals at R & R Auto salvage in Aurora, MO. And a very special thank you to Ed Witte for letting me photograph parts at his salvage yard CST also in Aurora, MO. Ed has a large section of Pontiac parts and can be reached by phone at 417-678-6994 or fax him a list of your wanted parts at 417-678-7305.

CONTENTS

Chapter 1: Decoding	5
Chapter 2: Front End Sheet Metal	12
Chapter 3: Doors and Outside Mirrors	27
Chapter 4: Quarter Panels and Rear End Sheet Metal	36
Chapter 5: Uni-Body and Roof	43
Chapter 6: Glass	47
Chapter 7: Nameplates	51
Chapter 8: Body Trim	64
Chapter 9: Interior Hardware	71
Chapter 10: Interior Trim and Accessories	81
Chapter 11: Electrical Accessories	91
Index	112

Chapter 1: Decoding Data Plates

Vehicle Identification Number

It is essential that you know how to decode the Vehicle Identification Number, know as VIN for short. This series of numbers and code letters indicates the model, and in later years the original type of powerplant.

Knowing how to decode the VIN can be useful in determining your car's authenticity, such as determining a real Trans Am from a mocked up Firebird, but can also be used in identifying the donor vehicle, sometimes parts were changed midyear and the VIN serial number can be used to determine this.

1967

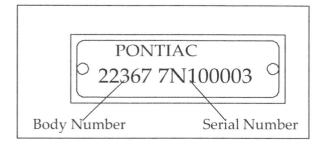

For 1967 models the VIN is found on a brightly plated tag that is attached to the hinge pillar of the driver's door. The format begins with the number '2' indicating the Pontiac line; this is followed by a four digit code for model and body style. Next will be the number '7' for the 1967 model year.

1967 Firebird Body Numbers

Code	Model	Model Year
22337	Firebird Hardtop	1967
22367	Firebird Convertible	1967

Seventh place indicates the assembly plant. N is for Norwood, and L for Van Nuys. The last digits are the basic serial number which begins at 100001 for each plant.

1968-1969

The format is the same as for the 1967 models, however the plate was now smaller, dull colored and moved to the top of the instrument panel on the driver's side readable through the windshield

1968-1969 Firebird Body Numbers

Code	Model	Model Year
22337	Firebird Hardtop	1968-69
22367	Firebird Convertible	1968-69

1968-1969 Firebird Body Numbers

Code	Assembly Plant
L	Van Nuys, A
N	Norwood, OH

1968-1969 Firebird Model Numbers

Code	Assembly Plant
8	1968
9	1969

1970-1971 MODELS

The location was the same as it was in 1969; however the format was changed slightly. It still began with the number '2' indicating the Pontiac line, but more codes for body numbers were added to represent the different models available, and since there was only a two-door hardtop now available all Firebirds will have the number '87' in the third and fourth digits of the VIN plate. This followed by the code for the model year, (0-1970 1-1971). This is followed by the assembly plant code, and ends with the basic serial number which begins at 100001 for each plant.

```
226871N1004
```

1970-1971 Firebird Body Numbers

Code	Model	Model Year
22387	Firebird	1970-71
22487	Esprit	1970-71
22687	Formula	1970-71
22887	Trans Am	1970-71

1972-1980 MODELS

The location was the same as it was in 1971 and still began with the number '2' indicating the Pontiac line. However the rest was changed. The second character is a single letter that indicates the car and model line, this is followed by the two digit code for body style; all Firebird models regardless of model were listed as the code '87 for two door hardtop.

2W87Z51007

1971-1980 Model Numbers

Code	Model	Year Used
2S87	Basic Firebird	1972-1981
2T87	Esprit	1972-1981
2U87	Formula	1972-1979
2V87	Trans Am	1972-1974
2V87	Formula	1980
2W87	Trans Am	1975-1980
2X87	10th Anniversary T/A	1979
2X87	Turbo Pace Car	1980

The fifth character in the VIN was a letter that represented the original engine. Note that the original engine may have been replaced at some point. The sixth digit of the VIN is the model year; this is followed by the code for assembly plant and the assembly line number. Again most plants began each model year at 100001, except the 1972 model year which began at 50001 at each plant.

1972-1981 V-8 Engine VIN Codes

Code	Engine	Years Used	Code	Engine	Years Used
M	350-ci 2-bbl S.E.	1972-1976	Z	400-ci 4-bbl	1976
N	350-ci 2-bbl D.E.	1972-1975	Y	301-ci 2-bbl	1977
R	400-ci 2-bbl S.E.	1972-1975	L	350-ci 4-bbl	1977-1979
T	400-ci 4-bbl D.E.	1972-1975	R	350-ci 4-bbl	1977-1979
X*	455-ci 4-bbl D.E.	1972-1975	X	350-ci 4-bbl	1977-1979
S	400-ci 4-bbl S.E.	1972-1975	Z	400-ci 4-bbl	1977-1979
Y	455-ci 4-bbl D.E.	1973-1975	K	403-ci 4-bbl	1977-1978
P	400-ci 2-bbl D.E.	1973-1975	U	305-ci 2-bbl	1978
J	350-ci 4-bbl	1976	W	301-ci 2-bbl V-8	1979-1981
H	350-ci 2-bbl	1976	Y	301-ci 2-bbl V-8	1979-1980
W	455-ci 4-bbl	1975-1976	G	305-ci 2-bbl V-8	1979-1981
H	350-ci 2-bbl	1976	H	305-ci 4-bbl V-8	1979-1981
P	350-ci 2-4-bbl	1976	K	403-ci 4-bbl V-8	1979
N	400-ci 2-bbl	1976	T	301-ci Turbo	1980-1981
			S	265-ci 2-bbl V-8	1980-1981

S.E.- Single Exhaust D.E. Dual Exhaust *- Super Duty

1981 MODELS

The VIN plate was still attached to the top of the driver's side instrument panel however an all new format was used. It will begin the country code '1' for USA, this is followed by the letter 'G' for General Motors, and the number '2' for the Pontiac line. The fourth character will be the letter 'A' for manual seat belts.

The fifth through the seventh is the model codes, refer to chart below for details. All Firebirds still only had one body style- a two door hardtop.

1981 Model Numbers

Code	Model	Year Used
2S87	Basic Firebird	1981
2T87	Esprit	1981
2V87	Formula	1981
2W87	Trans Am	1981

Eighth character represents the original engine refer to chart on page 6 for details. The check digit is in ninth position and usually has little to do with the interchange or even decoding the tag, it was for in factory only, model year is next. Plant code of either the 'N' for Norwood or L for Van Nuys is used. It ends with the six digit production sequence number which starts at each plant at 100001.

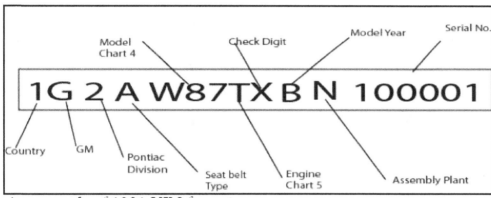

An example of 1981 VIN format

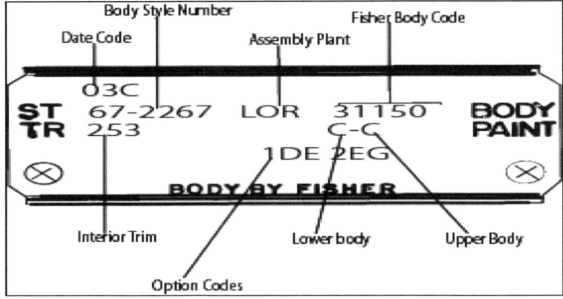
Typical 1967 Body tag

Fisher Body Tag

Attached to the firewall, usually on the driver's side, is the Fisher Body Tag. Like the VIN plate this plate too contains important information about the original trim and accessories that were installed on the car. Knowing how to decode this tag can be useful in finding the right shade or color of trim from a donor car. It can also be very useful in determining the model year when other identifying clues, such as the front end is missing.

Different formats were used, according to model year. But the basic information remains the same. Hidden in codes are the model year, assembly plant, exterior color and interior trim type and color. The build date is also represented here, but its location changes according to format. For 1967-early 1969 models the build date is the top line of information, while on later models the information is on the bottom line.

Regardless of the format you will see the letters ST or the word Style stamped into the tag. The last two digits of the model year, 67-1967, 68-1968 69-1969, 70-1970 and so on follows. Following this is the first five characters of the VIN, which is known as body number. However, we have seen variations of this code on early 1967 models. There have been codes such as 67-22637 and even 22437. The 22637 translate to a Custom Firebird with a V-8 and the 22437 as a Standard Firebird. The discrepancies appear to be because of their relation to the Camaro.

In the middle of this line is the assembly plant code; depending on the assembly plant this will either be a three-letter abbreviation or a single letter code that represents the factory. The numbers following this line is the Fisher body sequential number, and has nothing to do with the serial number that is shown in the VIN, they may or may not match. The letters BDY or the word Body will finish this line.

Below are the letters TRM or the word Trim. Following this is the interior trim code. By using our charts you will be able to decode your Firebird's trim style and color. Following this is the character code for the exterior color of the car. Since color doesn't affect interchange we have not listed these codes; for more information we suggest you obtain a copy of *Firebird Restoration 1967-1969* or *Trans Am Restoration 1970-1981* which are both available by the publisher.

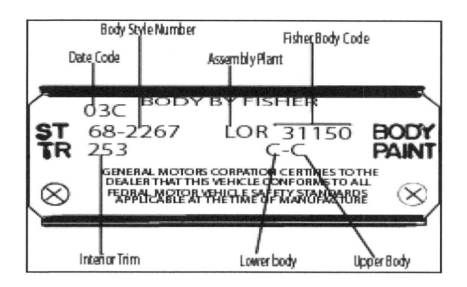

1967 Interior Trim Codes

Code	Color	Type	Code	Color	Type
250	Blue	Buckets	258	Red	Buckets
251	Gold	Buckets	259	Black	Buckets
252	Red	Buckets	260	Parchment	Bench
253	Black	Buckets	265	Blue	Bench
254	Parchment	Buckets	269	Black	Bench
255	Blue	Buckets	270	Blue	Bench
256	Turquoise	Bucket	271	Gold	Bench
			272	Black	Bench

1968 Interior Trim Codes

Code	Color	Code	Color	Code	Color
250	Teal	256	Turquoise	261	Turquoise
251	Gold	257	Gold	262	Parchment
252	Red	258	Red	269	Black
253	Black	259	Black	272	Black
255	Teal	260	Parchment	273	Parchment
				275	Parchment

1969 Interior Trim Codes

Code	Color	Code	Color	Code	Color
200	Blue	210	Blue	218	Black
202	Gold	212	Gold	227	Parchment
206	Green	214	Red	228	Black
207	Parchment	216	Green	249	Black
208	Black	217	Parchment	293	Gold*

1970 Interior Trim Codes

Code	Color	Code	Color	Code	Color
201	Dark Blue	211	Dark Blue	217	Sandalwood
203	Dark Saddle	212	Ivory	219	Black
206	Dark Jade	213	Dark Saddle	227	Sandalwood
207	Sandalwood	214	Dark Sienna	229	Black
209	Black	216	Dark Jade		

All are Bucket Seats #- Cloth/vinyl trim

1971 Interior Trim Codes

Code	Color	Code	Color	Code	Color
201	Dark Blue	211	Dark Blue	217	Sandalwood
203	Dark Saddle	212	Ivory	219	Black
206	Dark Jade	213	Dark Saddle	227	Sandalwood
207	Sandalwood	214	Dark Sienna	229	Black
209	Black	216	Dark Jade		

1972 Interior Trim Codes

Code	Color	Code	Color	Code	Color
121	Ivory	211	Dark Blue	251	Lt. Beige
131	Dark Saddle	221	Ivory	261	Black
141	Dark Green	231	Dark Saddle	351	Lt. Beige#
161	Black	241	Dark green	361	Black#

All are Bucket Seats #- Cloth/vinyl trim

1973 Interior Trim Codes

Code	Color	Code	Color	Code	Color
232	White	236	Black	243	Saddle
233	Saddle	242	White	246	Black
				247	Oxblood
				255	Beige#

All are Bucket Seats #- Cloth/vinyl trim

1974 Interior Trim Codes

Code	Color	Code	Color	Code	Color
572	White	583	Saddle #	592	White
573	Saddle	586	Black #	593	Saddle
576	Black	590	Red	594	Green
				596	Black

All are Bucket Seats #- Cloth/vinyl trim

1975 Interior Trim Codes

Code	Color	Code	Color	Code	Color
11V	White	19V	Black	26W	Blue
11W	White	19W	Black	63V	Saddle
				63W	Saddle
				73W	Oxblood

All are all vinyl bucket seats

1976 Interior Trim Codes

Code	Color	Code	Color	Code	Color
11N	White	19M	Black	91M, 91N*	Blue
11M*	White	19N*	Black	63N 64M*	Buckskin
				71M,71N*	Firethrone
				• Custom	

1977 Interior Trim Codes

Code	Color	Code	Color	Code	Color
11N	White	62 R, 62N 62B#	Dark Camel	24N, 92N	Blue
11M	White	19 R 19N 19B#	Black	74R,71N,71B#	Carmine

#-Cloth and vinyl

1978 Interior Trim Codes

Code	Color	Code	Color	Code	Color
11R	White	19M	Black	91M, 91N*	Blue
11N	White	19N* 19B#	Black	63N 64M*	Buckskin
				71M,71N* 91R	Firethrone
				71 R 71B#	

1979 Interior Trim Codes

Code	Color	Code	Color	Code	Color
12R	Oyster	19R, 19N, 19B#	Black	24N 24B#	Blue
12N	Oyster	62R, 62N, 62B#	Dark Camel	74R,74n,74B#	Dark carmine
152	Silver			# cloth and vinyl	

1980 Interior Trim Codes

Code	Color	Code	Color	Code	Color
12R	Oyster	19R, 19N, 19B#	Black	26B#,26 D	Blue
12N	Oyster	62,D 62R, 62N, 62B#	Dark Camel	26 N, 26R	
12C#					
74R, 74N,74B#	Dark Carmine			# cloth and vinyl	

1981 Interior Trim Codes

Code	Color	Code	Color	Code	Color
15V 15W	Silver	19N	Black	26B#, 26D,26N, 26R	Blue
63B	Light Sandstone	64B#,64D 64N, 64R	Saddle	75R,75N, 75B	Red

Chapter 2: Front End Sheet Metal

Hood

Several different types of hoods were used on the Firebird and a very popular interchange is swapping a Formula hood over to a Plain-Jane Firebird, or to a lesser degree the Trans Am hood. Each hood has its own characteristics and interchange range. A plain unadorned hood has more interchange range than the sport style hoods like the Trans Am and Formula due to their design.

When looking at a hood take into consideration the options that are installed on the car. For example the hood mounted tachometer requires a special opening be cut out on the underside of the hood. When inspecting a hood, take a careful look at the edges the corners are easily bent, so make sure they are straight. Also make sure the hood is a not warped, a lightweight hood like the Trans Am unit are more prone to being bent in the middle. Check any chrome trim on the hood that your car is not originally equipped with, if you don't want to use the trim you will have to fill the holes, which can add to the expense of your hood.

Note all interchanges listed here are on the bare hood, without nameplates, trim or hinges. These factors may affect your interchange. For example: the same hood may be used, but the nameplates may be in a different location. Also be careful of the interchanges. Sometimes a hood from another model will fit, but only if you use the other model's hinges. So be sure to correctly read the interchange or you may end up with a hood that will not bolt to your Firebird's hinges.

Note how the hood is cut out to provide room for the hood-mounted tachometer.

1967

Base Firebird..................................1

400-ci..2

1968

Base Firebird..................................4

400-ci..3

1969

Base Firebird..................................4

400-ci

Except Ram Air or Trans Am................3

Ram Air..6

Trans Am..5

1970-72

Base Firebird..................................7

Esprit..7

Formula

Dummy hood scoops........................8

Functional hood scoops.....................9

Trans Am.......................................10

1973-75

Base Firebird..................................11

Esprit..11

Formula

Dummy hood scoops........................12

Functional hood scoops.....................15

Trans Am.......................................13

1976

Base Firebird.................................. 11

Esprit.. 11

Formula... 14

Trans Am....................................... 13

1977-1979

Base Firebird.................................. 16

Esprit.. 16

Formula... 17

Trans Am....................................... 18

1980-1981

Base Firebird.................................. 16

Esprit.. 16

Without Turbo Hood

Formula... 17

Trans Am....................................... 18

With Turbo Hood

Formula... 19

Trans Am....................................... 19

Interchange Number: 1
Part Number: 978846
Type: Standard
Usage: 1967 Firebird, except with 400-ci V-8.
Notes: Interchange Number 2 will fit

Interchange Number: 2
Part Number: 9789418
Type: Sports
Usage: 1967 Firebird 400-ci
Notes: Interchange Number 3 will fit

Interchange Number: 3
Part Number: 9793430
Type: Sports
Usage: 1968-69 Firebird with a 400-ci V-8, Except Ram Air or Trans Am.

Interchange Number 4
Part Number: 9793429
Type: Standard
Usage: 1968-69 Firebird, except with 400-ci V-8.
Notes: Will fit interchange number 1

Trans Am model used a special hood all years. Shown is the 1969 model.

Interchange Number: 5
Part Number: 546014
Type: Trans Am
Usage: 1969 Firebird Trans Am.

Interchange Number 6
Part Number: 9797763
Type: Ram Air
Usage: 1969 Firebird, 400-ci H.O. or Ram Air. V-8.
Notes: To fit to non- Ram Air models will require additional parts. Cable, air cleaner, etc.

Interchange Number: 7
Part Number: 478940
Type: Standard
Usage: 1970-72 Firebird, except Formula or Trans Am models.

Interchange Number: 8
Part Number: 480172
Type: Formula
Usage: 1970-72 Firebird Formula with dummy hood scoops.

Interchange Number: 9
Part Number: 479677
Type: Formula
Usage: 1970-72 Firebird Formula with functional hood scoops.

Interchange Number: 10
Part Number: 481845
Type: Trans Am
Usage: 1970-72 Firebird Trans Am.

Interchange Number: 11
Part Number: 500085
Type: Standard
Usage: 1973-76 Firebird, except Trans Am or Formula
Notes: this hood will fit interchange number 7.

Interchange Number: 12
Part Number: 490660
Type: Formula
Usage: 1973-75 Firebird Formula, without functional hood scoops.
Notes: Will fit Interchange Number 8

Interchange Number: 13
Part Number: 500154
Type: Shaker
Usage: 1973-76 Firebird Formula or Trans Am with Shaker Hood.

Interchange Number: 14
Part Number: 499976
Type: Formula
Usage: 1976 Firebird Formula, without functional hood scoops
Notes: Due to hood creases will not fit other models.

Interchange Number: 15
Part Number: 490661
Type: Formula
Usage: 1973-75 Firebird Formula, with functional hood scoops
Notes: Will fit interchange number 9. Due to hood creases will not 1976 models.

Interchange Number: 16
Part Number: 10011150
Type: Standard
Usage: 1977-1981 Firebird, except Formula or Trans Am.

Interchange Number: 17
Part Number: 10012180
Type: simulated hood scoops
Usage: 1977-1981 Firebird Formula except with turbo hood.

Interchange Number: 18
Part Number: 10011151
Type: Shaker hood
Usage: 1977-1981 Firebird with Trans Am package except turbo.

Interchange Number: 19
Part Number: 10014554
Type: turbo hood
Usage: 1980-1981 Firebird with turbo charger.

1970-1972 Trans Am Shaker hood, inspect the edge of the hood for signs of damage, also make sure the edges are straight.

Note the underside of the Shaker scoop and the rolled down edges indicating it is a factory hood.

Hinges, Hood

1967-1969

All models.....................1

1970

All models.....................2

1971-75

All models.....................3

Interchange Number: 1
  Part Number: 3910667- Left 3910668- Right
  Usage: 1967-69 Firebird, Camaro; 1965-67 Chevelle, full-size Chevrolet; 1966-67 Chevy II.

Interchange Number: 2
  Part Number: 9790524- Left 9790525- Right
  Usage: 1970 Firebird, Camaro

Interchange Number: 3
  Part Number: 14034129- Left:
  14034130- Right
  Usage: 1971-81 Firebird except Turbo Charged models; 1971-1981, Camaro
  Notes: Will fit Interchange number 2; but Interchange number 2 will not fit here.

The Shaker hood will fit other models but require the shaker air cleaner and other accessories to make the interchange functional.

Hood Springs

1967-1969

Except 400-ci 4-bbl..........................1
400-ci 4-bbl....................................2

1970

All..1

1971-1973

All..3

1974-1981

All..4

Interchange Number: 1
  Part Number: 3848272
  Usage: 1967-70 Firebird, except 1969 400-ci 4-bbl; 1964-72 Tempest; 1969-70 full-size Pontiac; 1964-65 Chevelle, all models; 1966-67 Chevelle SS 396; 1971-72 Chevelle with domed hood; 1967-69 Camaro SS; 1965-66 full-size Chevrolet; 1970 full-size Chevrolet; 1971-72 Monte Carlo; 1972 El Camino, Sprint; 1964-72 F85/Cutlass.

Interchange Number: 2
  Part Number: 546325
  Usage: 1969 Firebird, 400-ci 4-bbl.

Interchange Number: 3
  Part Number: 3907626
  Usage: 1971-73 Firebird; 1970 Monte Carlo; 1970-1973 Camaro.

Interchange Number: 4
  Part Number: 14034133
  Usage: 1974-81 Firebird, all models 1974-1981 Camaro.

Hood Latch

1967

All...1

1968

All...2

1969

All...3

1970

All...4

1971-1981

All...5

Interchange Number: 1
   Part Number: 9712100
   Usage: 1967 Firebird, all models.

Interchange Number: 2
   Part Number: 9715566
   Usage: 1968 Firebird, all models.

Interchange Number: 3
   Part Number: 9718500
   Usage: 1969 Firebird, all models.

Interchange Number: 4
   Part Number: 97121788
   Usage: 1970 Firebird, Tempest, all models.

Interchange Number: 5
   Part Number: 9857248
   Usage: 1971-81 Firebird, all models; 1971-72 Tempest, LeMans, with chrome bumper only.

Fenders

Front fenders are a very popular used parts buy, and can be a good deal over brand new sheet metal. There are cost savings; it costs less to buy a used fender than it does to buy the fender in new metal. The other; in some cases it may be the only way to buy the item, not all sheet metal is reproduced, and GM is no longer producing some pieces.

When buying a used fender you should check its overall condition, you should look for any signs of damage such as a dent or scrapes. Be sure to check the backside of the fender and the inner radius of the wheel well, which are areas where rust is likely to form, it can also indicate signs of previous repairs. You should also lightly tap the fender and poke the metal along the edges, especially the area at the bottom of the fender, just behind the wheel opening. If you feel the metal give or if it feels weak reject the fender. This is a sign of rust, and repairing a rusted out fender is a last resort option only.

Also while tapping on the fender, listen for a dull thud sound, which can indicate a repair that was done with plastic filler. It might also be a wise idea to run a small magnet over the fender, to check for this. Any signs of plastic filler repair should make you reject the fender or at least be aware of the extra work.

Check the trim and accessories on the fender, it should match your car's or should have none. It is easier to drill holes than fill them; also make sure accessories are included, such as the Trans Am fender insets. Trim should be part of your inspection; but it is not included in our interchange. All interchanges listed here are a plain fender without any trim.

1967

All.. 1

1968

All.. 1

1969

Except Trans AM............................. 2

Trans Am... 3

1970

Except Trans Am.............................. 4

Trans Am... 5

1971

Except Trans Am.............................. 6

Trans Am... 5

1972

Except Trans Am.............................. 7

Trans Am... 5

1973-1975

Except Trans Am.............................. 7

Trans Am... 8

1976

Except Trans Am.............................. 9

Trans Am... 10

1977-1981

Except Trans Am.............................. 11

Trans Am... 12

Interchange Number: 1
  Part Number: 9793816 Right 973817 Left
  Usage: 1967-68 Firebird, all models.

Interchange Number: 2
  Part Number: 9798212 Right 97898213 Left
  Usage: 1969 Firebird, except Trans Am.

Interchange Number: 3
  Part Number: 546680 Right 546681 Left
  Usage: 1969 Firebird Trans Am.

Interchange Number: 4
  Part Number: 478612 Right 478613 Left
  Usage: 1970 Firebird, except Trans Am

Interchange Number: 5
  Part Number: 480898 Right 408099 Left
  Usage: 1970-72 Firebird Trans Am

Interchange Number: 6
  Part Number: 483512 Right 483513 Left
  Usage: 1971 Firebird, except Trans Am

Interchange Number: 7
  Part Number: 492991 Right 492992 Left
  Usage: 1972-75 Firebird, except Trans Am

Interchange Number: 8
  Part Number: 492993 Right 492994 Left
  Usage: 1973-75 Firebird, Trans Am Notes: Will fit Interchange Number 5.

Interchange Number: 9
  Part Number: 546936 Right 546937 Left
  Usage: 1976 Firebird, except Trans Am

Interchange Number: 10
  Part Number: 546938 Right 546939 Left
  Usage: 1976 Firebird Trans Am

Interchange Number: 11
  Part Number: 526147 Right 526146 Left
  Usage: 1977-1981 Firebird, except Trans Am

Interchange Number: 12
  Part Number: 10004690 Right 1004691 Left
  Usage: 1977-1981 Firebird Trans Am

Fender, Skirts

1967

All.. 1

1968

All.. 2

1969

All.. 3

1970-75

All.. 4

Interchange Number: 1
  Part Number: 9777835 Right 9777836 Left
  Usage: 1967 Firebird, all models

Interchange Number: 2
  Part Number: 9792120 Right 9792121 Left
  Usage: 1968 Firebird, all models

Interchange Number: 3
  Part Number: 9796531 Right 9796532 Left
  Usage: 1969 Firebird, all models

Interchange Number: 4
  Part Number: 478112 Right 478113 Left
  Usage: 1970-75 Firebird, all models

Interchange Number: 5
  Part Number: 10010933 Right 100109934 Left
  Usage: 1976-1981 Firebird, all models

Front Fender, Air Extractors, Louvers and Extensions

Though this part is a good buys as used parts, you must use care in inspecting them as some like the front valance receives abuse during its life. This is the panel that runs below the front bumper and is what the spoiler is mounted to. Keep this in mind; the panels were drilled to accept the spoiler. No special panels were made only for the cars with a spoiler. Thus you can use a valance from a car without a spoiler on a car with a spoiler; you just have to drill the holes, but to use one from a car with a spoiler on a car without spoiler you will have to fill the holes first. A general inspection is all that it takes to view this part; watch for signs of damage and rust.

1967

Front Valance...1

1968

Front Valance...2

1969

Front valance...3
Air vents
Except Trans Am
  Upper..7
  Lower..8
Trans Am..9

1970

Front valance................................. 4
Air Vents
Trans Am..6

1971

Front valance................................. 4
Air Vents
Except Trans Am............................10
Trans Am..6

1972-1973

Front valance................................. 4
Air Vents
Trans Am..6

1974-1975

Front valance 5
Air Vents
Trans Am..6

1976-1981

Front valance ....part of bumper
Air Vents
Trans Am..6

Interchange Number: 1
  Part Number: 9789297
  Usage: 1967 Firebird, all models

Interchange Number: 2
  Part Number: 9792108
  Usage: 1968 Firebird, all models

Interchange Number: 3
  Part Number: 9796087
  Usage: 1969 Firebird, all models with steel valance.

Interchange Number: 4
  Part Number: 480628
  Usage: 1970-73 Firebird, all models

Interchange Number: 5
  Part Number: Varies with color
  Usage: 1974-75 Firebird.
  Notes: These panels are molded in color to match the exterior of the car. Your best bet is to find a matching color or paint it to match.

Interchange Number: 6
Part Number: 480797 Left hand 480796 Right hand
Part: Fender vents
Usage: 1970-81 Trans Am
Notes: These panels are molded in color to match the exterior of the car. Your best bet is to find a matching color or paint it to match.

Interchange Number: 7
Part Number: 9796361 Left hand 9796362 Right hand
Part: Fender vents, upper
Usage: 1969 Firebird, except Trans Am

Interchange Number: 8
Part Number: 9796363 Left hand 9796364 Right hand
Part: Fender vents, lower
Usage: 1969 Firebird, except Trans Am

Interchange Number: 9
Part Number: 546251 Left hand 546252 Right hand
Part: Fender vents,
Usage: 1969 Trans Am

Interchange Number: 10
Part Number: *483915* Left hand *483916* Right hand
Part: Fender vents,
Usage: 1971 Firebird ,except Trans Am

A front Valance panel, is just below the front bumper and supports the front turn lamps, on some models.

1969 Firebird simulated air vents.

Radiator Support and Baffle
1967-1969

All……………………………………………….1

1970-1975

All……………………………………………….2

1976-1981

All……………………………………………….3

Interchange Number: 1
Part Number: 3962940
Usage: 1967-1969 Firebird, all models.

Interchange Number: 2
Part Number: 477971
Usage 1970-1975 Firebird, all V-8 models or six cylinders with heavy duty cooling.

Interchange Number: 3
Part Number: 10010664
Usage 1976 Firebird, all V-8 models or six cylinders with heavy duty cooling; 1977-1981 Firebird all models
Note some are a two part design with separate brace.

Grilles

Buying a used grille may be the only way to get the part you need. However, you can also save a great deal of money by purchasing a used grille.

Many different components make up the grille assembly, and many of them like nameplates and trim are covered elsewhere in this guide. The interchangeable parts we are discussing here are the grille screen and frame. However, on 1967 and 1968 models there is an insert that is placed between the head lamps to give the car a full-width grille featured appearance and these inserts are covered here in this section.

Before you remove the grille inserts, if they are still mounted in the car; inspect the grille fins, the plastic is easily broken. Also check the plastic for signs of pitting or any repairs, such as a fin that will not line up. Next, check the frame making sure it is free of cracks and is not broken. Be sure to check the back of the grill under the hood for any signs of damage, or repainting.

REMOVING GRILLES

1967-1972

Each grille unit is held in place to the front bumper with four ¼-14x3/4 inch hex head taps, u-nuts and brackets. To remove you will need a socket driver with a compatible socket, a pair of pliers or vise grips may also come in handy. Remove the taps from the grille and pull the grille frame free from the bumper.

1973

Mounts similar to the earlier models. However, they use a special bracket at the bottom of the grille frame. This bracket is attached to the car, and is best that it is removed with the grille. This bracket is no longer made and is hard to find as it was used this year only. This bracket attaches to the back of the nosepiece with 5/8 inch long ¼ inch hex head screws, and u-nuts. So make sure you keep the location of the screws marked. Also be sure to carefully check the extension on the grille frame, where the bracket mounts. This area is more prone to stress fractures.

1974-76

The twin grille units here are held in place with #8-18x3/4 inch hex head screws and 3/16 inch stamped nuts and u-nuts. Note that the grille inserts mount from the backside of the nosepiece and have to be removed in this matter. You cannot simply pull the inserts free from the front of the car.

1977-1978

The twin grille units are placed and removed from the front of the car; they are held in place with screws and u-nuts. To remove you must support the u-nut so that it will not turn when removing the screws. When the screws are removed you simply pull the insert away from the car.

1979-1981

The twin grille units are placed at the bottom of the front bumper and held in place with screw and u-nuts to remove you must support the u-nut so that it will not turn when removing the screws. When the screws are removed you simply pull the insert away from the car.

MAKING A GRILLE WORK

A common trend in the 1960's and 1970's was to place a flat black grille on the sports type car giving it a racecar edge look. In most cases the inserts were the same pattern, only the finish was the difference. In these cases, which are marked in the interchange section under notes, you can use a more common Firebird grille, repaint it and use it on your Trans Am or Formula models.

Start by cleaning the grille unit with a mild soapy water bath and then rinse thoroughly, allow to dry. Before you do anything else wipe the unit down with wax and grease remover. This will remove the invisible presence of wax and grease that could spoil your paint job.

Next lightly sand the exposed areas with 400 grit sand paper. Don't use excessive pressure and sand into the plastic, just enough so that it will give the paint a surface to bite into. Again, carefully wipe the grille down with wax and grease remover and a tack cloth and then apply two light coats of good quality flat black enamel. To get a good overall appearance, it is best to hang the grille assembly up on a fishing line so you can move it about and get it from all sides. Allow the assembly to dry over night before attempting to install it on your Firebird.

1967

Insert

Except 400...1

400-ci..2

Headlamp... 3

1968
Insert
Except 400.................................. 4
400-ci.. 5
Headlamp....................................3

1969
Insert
Silver..6
Black..7

1970-71
Insert
   Silver..8
   Black...9

1972
Insert
   Silver..10
   Black...11

1973
Insert
   Silver..12
   Black...13

1974
Insert
   Silver..14
   Black...15

1975
Insert
   Silver..16
   Black...17

1976
Insert
   All...18

1977
Insert
Except Formula or Trans Am............19
Formula or Trans Am.....................20

1978
Insert
Except Formula or Trans Am
Without Bluebird package...............21
Bluebird......................................24

Formula or Trans Am
Except Trans Am S.E....................22
Trans Am S.E..............................25

1979-1981
Insert
   All...23

The area between the headlamps on 1967 and 1968 Firebirds is a separate part. Both years use the same part number and will interchange.

Interchange Number: 1
   Part Number: 9788856 right 9788857-left
   Usage: 1967 Firebird, except 400-ci

Interchange Number: 2
   Part Number: 9789373 right 9789374 left
   Usage: 1967 Firebird, 400-ci

Interchange Number: 3
   Part Number: 9788858
   Usage: 1967-68 Firebird, all models
   Notes: Fits either side.

Interchange Number: 4
   Part Number: 9793725-right 9793726-left
   Usage: 1968 Firebird, except 400-ci

Interchange Number: 5
   Part Number: 9793723-right 9793724-left
   Usage: 1968 Firebird 400-ci.

Interchange Number: 6
   Part Number: 9795935-right 9795936-left
   Usage: 1969 Firebird except Trans Am.
   Notes: Silver

Interchange Number: 7
   Part Number: 546147-right 546148-left
   Usage: 1969 Firebird Trans Am.
   Notes: Interchange number 6 can be painted to fit here.

Interchange Number: 8
   Part Number: 478512-right 478513-left
   Usage: 1970-71 Firebird, except Formula 400 or Trans Am.

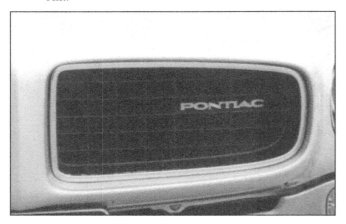

1970-1973 Firebird Grille design

1976 honey comb grille

Interchange Number: 9
   Part Number: 479690-right 479691-left
   Usage: 1970-71 Firebird Formula 400 or Trans Am.
   Notes: Interchange number 8 can be painted to fit here.

Interchange Number: 10
   Part Number: 485264-right 485265-left
   Usage: 1972 Firebird except Trans Am.
   Notes: Silver

Interchange Number: 11
   Part Number: 485575-right 485576-left
   Usage: 1972 Firebird except Trans Am.
   Notes: Black

Interchange Number: 12
   Part Number: 488965-right 488966-left
   Usage: 1973 Firebird except Trans Am or with Sports option.
   Notes: Silver

Interchange Number: 13
   Part Number: 491194-right 491195-left
   Usage: 1973 Firebird Trans Am or with sports option
   Notes: Black

Interchange Number: 14
   Part Number: 485546-right 485547-left
   Usage: 1974 Firebird except Trans Am or Formula package.
   Notes: Silver

Interchange Number: 15
   Part Number: 485552-right 485553-left
   Usage: 1974 Firebird Trans Am or Formula package.
   Notes: Black

Interchange Number: 16
   Part Number: 496286-right 496287-left
   Usage: 1975 Firebird except Trans Am or Formula package.
   Notes: Silver

Interchange Number: 17
   Part Number: 496284-right 496825-left
   Usage: 1975 Firebird Trans Am or Formula package.
   Notes: Black

Interchange Number: 18
   Part Number: 498836-right 498835-left
   Usage: 1976 Firebird all models.
   Note: Paint to match.

Interchange Number: 19
   Part Number: 526089-right 526090-left
   Usage: 1977 Firebird, except Trans Am or Formula
   Notes: Gray

Interchange Number: 20
   Part Number: 526087-right 526088-left
   Usage: 1977 Firebird Trans Am or Formula
   Notes: Black

Interchange Number: 21
   Part Number: 549365-right 549366-left
   Usage: 1978 Firebird, except Trans Am or Formula
   Notes: Gray

Interchange Number: 22
   Part Number: 549946-right 549947-left
   Usage: 1978 Firebird Trans Am or Formula
   Notes: Black

Interchange Number: 23
   Part Number: 1001503-right 1001504-left
   Usage: 1979-1981 Firebird all models.
   Notes: Paint to match.

Interchange Number: 24
   Part Number: 549950-right 549951-left
   Usage: 1978 Firebird Esprit Bluebird package.

Interchange Number: 25
   Part Number: 549948-right 549949-left
   Usage: 1978 Trans Am Special Edition
   Notes: Gold Interchange Number 21 and 22 can be painted to match

1969 Firebird grille.

1977 Trans Am Special Edition model note the difference in the color of the frame.

1978 Trans Am without Special Edition Package.

1979-1981 grilles are easily removed after the screws are removed.

Front Bumper and Front End Panel

The front bumper on early models those up to 1974, also double as a front-end panel. When inspecting a bumper the bumper should be smooth and straight. Bent or dented bumpers are hard to repair and should be avoided. Small nicks and scratches are acceptable providing you are willing to have the bumper rechromed. If not, than the bumper should be free of all nicks and scrapes, a rare thing for a classic bumper.

Removing a bumper is hard; bolts will most likely be frozen and require WD-40 and lots of elbow grease. You may want to have a good solid large breaker bar handy. Also because of their weight it makes sense to have an extra pair of hands that are capable of holding the weight. This is especially true of the 1970-1973 models as the bumper is the whole front end of the car. The later model used a flexible nose cone, the actual bumper is a solid chunk of metal that is behind the unit.

1967-1968

Front Bumper

Except 400-ci………………………………1

400-ci……………………………………2

1969

Front Bumper

Outer, Left……………………………5
Center

Except 400-ci………………………………3

400-ci……………………………………4

Outer, Right……………………………5

1970-1972

Front Bumper……………………………6

1973

Front Bumper……………………………7

1974-1975

Front Bumper……………………………8

1976

Front Bumper……………………………9
Nose Panel………………………………10

1977-1978

Front Bumper……………………………11
Nose Panel………………………………12

1979-1981

Front Bumper……………………………13
Nose Panel………………………………14

Interchange Number: 1
Part Number: 9788848
Usage: 1967-68 Firebird except 400-ci V-8

Interchange Number: 2
Part Number: 9789777
Usage: 1967-68 Firebird 400-ci V-8

Interchange Number: 3
Part Number: 9797454
Usage: 1969 Firebird except 400-ci V-8
Notes: Bright center

Interchange Number: 4
Part Number: 9795649
Usage: 1969 Firebird 400-ci V-8
Notes: Bright center

Interchange Number: 5
Part Number: 9784320 right 9784321 left
Usage: 1969 Firebird, all models
Notes: Outer bars, originally colored to match car, Can be painted to match.

Interchange Number: 6
Part Number: 477705
Usage: 1970-72 Firebird, all models
Notes: Paint to match

Interchange Number: 7
Part Number: 488410
Usage: 1973 Firebird, all models
Notes: Paint to match

Interchange Number: 8
   Part Number: 4498472
   Usage: 1974-75 Firebird, all models
   Notes: Paint to match

Interchange Number: 9
   Part Number: 499500
   Usage: 1976 Firebird, all models
   Notes: Faceplate

Interchange Number: 10
   Part Number: 526351
   Usage: 1976 Firebird, all models
   Notes: Nose panel

Interchange Number: 11
   Part Number: 525761
   Usage: 1977-1978 Firebird, all models
   Notes: Bumper bar

Interchange Number: 12
   Part Number: 547092
   Usage: 1977-1978 Firebird, all models
   Notes: Nose panel

Interchange Number: 13
   Part Number: 10005812
   Usage: 1979-1981 Firebird, all models
   Notes: Faceplate

Interchange Number: 14
   Part Number: 10004629
   Usage: 1979-1981 Firebird, all models
   Notes: Nose panel

The difference between a regular and a 400-ci cars front bumper. Firebirds with a 400-ci power plant used this medallion.

Spoiler, Front

Because of their composition and the very nature of the front spoiler this item is easily damaged. So make sure you give them a careful inspection before buying. Be extra careful around lower edges and the mounting areas it is these areas that get the most abuse. Spoilers were first introduced as an option in 1969, where part number 546573 found its way on to the Trans Am and other models. It was just a simple black colored panel. From 1970-1975 the spoilers were molded in body color, but can be painted to match; part numbers are given are for white. After 1975 the spoilers had to be painted to match the car. The 1970-1979 models consisted of a three piece design. The center spoiler and the outer wheel flares.

1970-1975
Center Spoiler..................................1
Flares..4

1976-1978
Center Spoiler..................................2
Flares..5

1979-1981
Center Spoiler..................................3
Flares..6

Interchange Number: 1
   Part Number: 481629 (white)
   Center Spoiler
   Usage: 1970-1975 Firebird, all models

Interchange Number: 2
   Part Number: 10006809
   Center Spoiler
   Usage: 1979-1981 Firebird, all models

Interchange Number: 3
   Part Number: 10005779
   Center Spoiler
   Usage: 1975-1978 Firebird, all models

Interchange Number: 4
   Part Number: 483889 Right 483890 Left (white)
   Fender Flares
   Usage: 1970-1975 Firebird, all models

Interchange Number: 5
   Part Number: 526825 Right 526826 Left
   Fender Flares
   Usage: 1976-1978 Firebird, all models

Interchange Number: 6
   Part Number: 10006865 Right 10006866 Left
   Fender Flares
   Usage: 1976-1978 Firebird, all models

Chapter 3: Doors and Outside Mirrors

Door Shells

Check the door over carefully, looking for signs of damage and repairs in the same manner that is discussed under the fender section (see Chapter 2). Rust is also an enemy of doors and the most common place for rust is the bottom of the door, as dirt and leaves get into the door and blocks the drains. Be sure to pull the inner door panel, if the door has one installed, and check out the condition of the inner shell again. Look in the bottom of the door for signs of rust, this way requires a flash light, a small one with a bright beam works better than a big one, also check out the area around the door handle.

Our interchange listed here is based on a bare door shell, stripped of all its trim, door handle window glass and window regulators. This is done to give more interchange range, as glass can affect the interchange between body styles.

1967

All..1

1968

Left

Early..3

Late..4

Right..2

1969

All..5

1970

All..6

1971

All..7

1972

All..8

1973-1974

All..9

1975-1981

All..10

Interchange Number: 1
   Part Number: 7645892 Right 7645893 Left
   Usage: 1967 Firebird, Camaro, all body styles.

Interchange Number: 2
   Part Number: 7742292 Right
   Usage: 1968 Firebird, Camaro, all body styles.

Interchange Number: 3
   Part Number: 7779693 Left
   Usage: 1968 Firebird, Camaro, all body styles.
   Notes: First generation style round mirror.

Interchange Number: 4
   Part Number: 7742293 Left
   Usage: 1968 Firebird, Camaro, all body styles.
   Notes: Second generation style rectangular shaped mirror.

Interchange Number: 5
   Part Number: 8723785 right 8723745 left
   Usage: 1969 Firebird; 1969 Camaro right-hand side only. All body styles.
   Notes: Salvage Yard dealers say left -hand door from Camaro will fit if you use Camaro's mirror.

Interchange Number: 6
   Part Number: 9804220 right 9804221 left
   Usage: 1970 Firebird
   Note: Camaro door will not fit

Interchange Number: 7
   Part Number: 9863006 right 9863007 left
   Usage: 1971 Firebird
   Note: Will fit Interchange number 7. Camaro door will not fit.

Interchange Number: 8
   Part Number: 9604462 right 9604463 left
   Usage: 1972 Firebird
   Note: Will fit Interchanges number 7, 8 Camaro door will not fit

Interchange Number: 9
　Part Number: 9645412 right 9645413 left
　Usage: 1973-1974 Firebird
　Note: Will fit Interchanges 1, 8 and 9.
　Camaro door will not fit

Interchange Number: 10
　Part Number: 20162368 right 20162369 left
　Usage: 1975-1981 Firebird
　Note: Camaro door will not fit. Will fit earlier models, but must use 1975-81 inner door handle and door panel.

Door Hinge

1967

Upper...1

Lower...5

1968

Upper...2

Lower...6

1969

Upper...3

Lower...7

1970-1981

Upper...4

Lower...8

Interchange Number: 1
　Part Number: 7642529 (fits either side)
　Position: Upper
　Usage: 1967 Firebird, Camaro; 1966-67 Tempest, Chevelle, F85/Cutlass, Skylark.

Interchange Number: 2
　Part Number: 8736244 right 8736245 left
　Position: Upper
　Usage: 1968 Firebird, Camaro

Interchange Number: 3
　Part Number: 8736246 right 8736247 left
　Position: Upper
　Usage: 1969 Firebird, Camaro; 1969-79 Nova; 1971-77 Ventura II; 1977-79 Phoenix; 1975-1979 Skylark; 1976-79 Seville; 1973-79 Omega; 1973-75 Apollo

Interchange Number: 4
　Part Number: 1706370 right 1706371 left
　Position: Upper
　Usage: 1970-981 Firebird, Camaro; 1971-76 full-size Chevrolet; full-size Buick; full-size Oldsmobile; full-size Pontiac; 1971-76 Rivera; 1971-78 Toronado; 1971-76 Cadillac

Interchange Number: 5
　Part Number: 7683424 right 7683425 left
　Position: Lower
　Usage: 1967 Firebird, Camaro; 1966-67 Tempest, Chevelle F-85/Cutlass, Skylark.

Interchange Number: 6
　Part Number: 8736248 right 8736249 left
　Position: Lower
　Usage: 1968 Firebird, Camaro.

Interchange Number: 7
　Part Number: 9817408 right 9817409 left
　Position: Lower
　Usage: 1969 Firebird, Camaro; 1969-79 Novas; 1973-79 Omega; 1973-75 Apollo; 1977-79 Phoenix; 1975-79 Skylarks; 1976-79 Seville.

Interchange Number: 8
　Part Number: 9816926 right 9816927 left
　Position: Lower
　Usage: 1970-81 Firebird, Camaro; 1969-76 full-size Buick. Chevrolet, Pontiac, Oldsmobile, Cadillac; 1971-76 Rivera; 1971-78 Toronado.

Door Handle, Outside and Components

1967-1968

Handle..1

Button..4

1969

Handle..2

Button..5

1970-1981

Handle..3

Clip..6

Interchange Number: 1
　Part Number: 5716870 right 5716871 left
　Part: Outside door handle
　Usage: 1967-68 Firebird, All models and body styles; 1967-69 Camaro; 1968-74 Nova, all body styles, front and rear doors; 1960 Catalina six-widow sedan, wagon or Vista four-window sedan rear door handles only; 1960 Star Chief four-window sedan rear handles only; 1960 Bonneville four-window sedan or wagon rear door handles only. 1963-66 full-size Pontiac, all body styles front or rear doors; 1966-67 Tempest and LeMans four-door models or wagon, front door handles only; 1964-67 Chevelle all body styles, front door handles only. Interchange without button.
　Notes: Left-hand side handle in Interchange number two will fit.

Interchange Number: 2
　Part Number: 9706522 right 9706523 left
　Part: Outside door handle
　Usage: 1969 Firebird, All models and body styles; 1966-67 Tempest, LeMans and GTO 2-door models; 1966-67 Tempest and LeMans 4-door models, rear door handles only; 1968-69 Tempest and LeMans 4-door models, front door handles only. Interchange without button.

Interchange Number: 3
　Part Number: 20099254 right 20099255 left
　Part: Outside door handle
　Usage: 1970-1981 Firebird; 1971-1976 full-size Pontiac front and rear doors; 1975-1978 Astre (not Astre SJ); 1970-1981 Camaro; 1971-76 full-size Chevrolet front and rear doors.

Interchange Number: 4
　Part Number: 9709600
　Part: Outside door handle, button
　Usage: 1967-68 Firebird, Camaro

Interchange Number: 5
　Part Number: 97199686
　Part: Outside door handle, button
　Usage: 1969 Firebird, Camaro

Interchange Number: 6
　Part Number: 9711304
　Part: Outside door handle, clip
　Usage: 1970-1981 Firebird, Camaro; 1971-72 full-size Pontiac, Chevrolet.

Door Handle, Inside

1967

Handle

Std. Trim..1

Custom Trim....................................2

1968-1969

Handle

Std. Trim..4

Custom Trim....................................3

1970

Handle

Std. Trim..5

Custom Trim

First Type...6

Second Type....................................7

1971

Handle

Std. Trim..5

Custom Trim....................................7

1972-1974

Handle..7

1975-1981

Handle..8

Interchange Number: 1
Part Number: 4468414
Part: Inside door handle
Usage: 1967 Firebird except custom trims; 1966-67 Tempest, LeMans, GTO, Catalina, Executive, All models and body styles; 1965-67 Chevelle, Chevy II, Biscayne, Bel-Air; 1967 Camaro with standard interior trim.

Interchange Number: 2
Part Number: 7712035
Part: Inside door handle
Usage: 1967 Firebird, with Custom trim; 1967 Camaro with Custom interior trim.

Interchange Number: 3
Part Number: 7759094 right 7759095 left
Part: Inside door handle
Usage: 1968-69 Firebird, with Custom trim; 1968-69 Camaro with Custom interior trim.

Interchange Number: 4
Part Number: 7743521
Part: Inside door handle
Usage: 1968-69 Firebird, except Custom trim; 1968-69 Camaro except Custom interior trim; 1968-72 Tempest, LeMans, GTO; 1968-70 Catalina, Executive, with standard trim (Bonneville or Grand Prix will not fit); 1971-72 Nova with custom trim, rear doors only; 1968-72 Nova front doors only; 1970-72 Chevelle

Interchange Number: 5
Part Number: 9825238 right 9825239 left
Part: Inside door handle
Usage: 1970-71 Firebird, except Custom trim; 1970-74 Camaro, except with custom interior trim.

Interchange Number: 6
Part Number: 8801924 right 8801925 left
Part: Inside door handle
Usage: 1970 Firebird, with Custom trim; 1970 Bonneville and Grand Prix with Custom trim.
Notes: First type has no slots on escutcheon plate
Must use with this type of escutcheon plate

Interchange Number: 7
Part Number: 9836342 right 983643 left
Part: Inside door handle
Usage: 1970-71 Firebird, with Custom trim; 1970 Bonneville with Custom trim; 1970 Grand Prix with custom trim; 1971-72 Grand Prix, all; 1972-1974 Firebird, all.
Notes: Second type has 2 slots on escutcheon plate
Must use with this type of escutcheon plate

Interchange Number: 8
Part Number: 20347098 right 20347099 left
Part: Inside door handle
Usage: 1975-1981 Firebird, Camaro, Nova, Ventura II 1976-1981 Sunbird, Monza, Skyhawk two door coupe models only

Window Regulator Handle, Inside

1967

Handle

Std. Trim………………………………..1

Custom trim………………………………..2

1968

Handle…………………………………..3

1969

Handle…………………………………..4

1970-1975

Handle…………………………………..5

1976-1981

Handle…………………………………..6

Interchange Number: 1
Part Number: Varies with color
Part: Window regulator handle
Usage: 1967 Firebird with standard trim; 1967 Tempest front and rear door; 1967 Camaro with standard trim; 1967 Chevelle, full-size Chevrolet, Chevy II.

Interchange Number: 2
Part Number: Varies with color
Part: Window regulator handle
Usage: 1967 Firebird with custom trim; 1967 Camaro with custom trim.

Interchange Number: 3
Part Number: Varies with color
Part: Window regulator handle
Usage: 1968 Firebird, Tempest, LeMans, GTO, full-size Pontiac; 1968 Chevelle, Nova, full-size Chevrolet; 1968 Skylark, full-size Buick; 1968 F-85/Cutlass, full-size Oldsmobile.

Interchange Number: 4
Part Number: 8732961
Part: Window regulator handle
Usage: 1969 Firebird; 1969-70 Tempest, LeMans, GTO, full-size Pontiac; 1969-1971 Chevelle; 1969-1970 full-size Chevrolet; 1969-71 Skylark; 1969-70 full-size Buick; 1969-70 full-size- Oldsmobile; 1971 LeMans.

Interchange Number: 5
Part Number: 87322962
Part: Window regulator handle
Usage: 1970-75 Firebird; 1971 full-size Pontiac, Chevrolet, Buick, Oldsmobile.

Interchange Number: 6
Part Number: 20037597
Part: Window regulator handle
Usage: 1976-81 Firebird; 1976-1981 full-size Pontiac, Chevrolet, Buick, Oldsmobile, Nova, Ventura II, Monte Carlo, Grand Prix

Window Regulator and Motor

1967

Manual

Std. Trim...1

Custom trim......................................2

Power..8

Motor..9

1968-1969

Manual

Std. Trim...3

Custom trim......................................4

Power..7

Motor..9

1970-1975

Manual..5

Power..6

Motor..9

1976-1981

Manual..5

Power..6

Motor..10

Interchange Number: 1
Part Number: 7681466 right 7681467 left
Part: Window regulator, Manual
Usage: 1967 Firebird, except Custom trim; 1967 Camaro except custom trim.

Interchange Number: 2
Part Number: 7651903 right 7651904 left
Part: Window regulator, Manual
Usage: 1967 Firebird, with Custom trim; 1967 Camaro with custom trim.

Interchange Number: 3
Part Number: 7740411 right 7740412 left
Part: Window regulator, Manual
Usage: 1968-69 Firebird, with standard trim; 1968-69 Camaro with standard trim.

Interchange Number: 4
Part Number: 7726801 right 7726802 left
Part: Window regulator, Manual
Usage: 1968-69 Firebird, with custom trim; 1968-69 Camaro with custom trim.

Interchange Number: 5
Part Number: 20041528 right 20041529 left
Part: Window regulator, Manual
Usage: 1970-1981 Firebird; 1970-81 Camaro, except custom trim or 1973-1974 Type LT.

Interchange Number: 6
Part Number: 20041548 right 20041549 left
Part: Window regulator, Power
Usage: 1970-1981 Firebird with power windows; 1975-1981 Camaro with power windows.
Notes: Units from 1970-74 Camaro will not fit.

Interchange Number: 7
Part Number: 9712928 right 9712929 left
Part: Window regulator, Power
Usage: 1968-69 Firebird with power windows; 1968-69 Camaro with power windows.

Interchange Number: 8
Part Number: 9709128 right 9709129 left
Part: Window regulator, Power
Usage: 1967 Firebird with power windows; 1967 Camaro with power windows.

Interchange Number: 9
Part Number: 5045587 right 5045588 left
Part: Motor, window regulator
Usage: 1967-75 Firebird with power windows; 1962-64 full-size Pontiac 4-dr. hardtop; 1966-75 full-size Pontiac with power windows, front and rear doors; 1970-75 Grand Prix; 1969-75 Tempest, LeMans 2-dr hardtop and convertible 1965-74 full-size Chevrolet except coupe; 1966-75 Chevelle coupe; 1967-75 Camaro; 1970-75 Chevelle, Monte Carlo, full-size Chevrolet-front doors only.

Interchange Number: 10
Part Number: 4999678 right 4999680 left
Part: Motor, window regulator
Usage: 1976-1977 Firebird, Camaro, Lemans, Grand Prix Monet Carlo, with power windows front windows only.

Door Lock, and Components

1967
Lock..1

1968
Lock..2

1969
Lock..3

1970-1972
Lock..4

1974-1977
Lock..5
Actuator..6

1978-1981
Lock..5
Actuator..7

Interchange Number: 1
Part Number: 7648724 right 7648725 left
Part: Door lock
Usage: 1967 Firebird, Camaro

Interchange Number: 2
Part Number: 7740484 right 7740485 left
Part: Door lock
Usage: 1968 Firebird, Camaro

Interchange Number: 3
Part Number: 8720401 right 8720402 left
Part: Door lock
Usage: 1969 Firebird, Camaro; 1968-70 Nova

Interchange Number: 4
Part Number: 9801701 right 9801702 left
Part: Door lock
Usage: 1970-72 Firebird, Camaro
Notes: Interchange number 5 will fit.

Interchange Number: 5
Part Number: 1748553 right 1748554 left
Part: Door lock
Usage: 1973-1981 Firebird, Camaro

Interchange Number: 6
Part Number: 9633793 right 9633794 left
Part: Door lock actuator
Usage: 1973-1977 Firebird, Camaro

Interchange Number: 7
Part Number: 22020256 either side
Part: Door lock actuator
Usage: 1978-1981 Firebird, Camaro

Standard round mirror for 1968

With chrome plated mirrors make sure the chrome is smooth and free of rust and pits. It doesn't make economical sense to have a mirror assembly rechromed, when you can find another unit that is in better shape. Most mirrors have a large interchange base, so you have a large lot to choose from.

A remote control mirror is important to also check the condition of the remote control cable. A bent or damage cable can cause the mirror not to work and be worthless.

Standard rectangular mirror for 1969

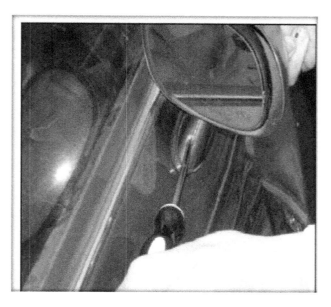

Most mirrors are held on with a single screw at the base.

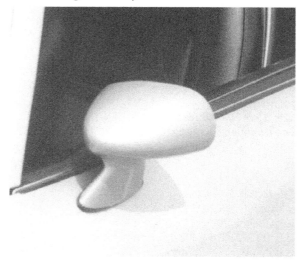

Custom sport mirror for Firebird has to be repainted. Shown is the 1973-75 version. It can fit 1970-72 models.

Mirror, Outside Rear View

All mirrors should be checked over for damage. Make sure the head moves freely, but that the mirror will stay in place. These are the two biggest factors to watch for when buying a used mirror. A broken mirror glass is not that much of a concern, unless you're going for date coding, as it can be easily replaced at your local glass and mirror shop.

1977 style racing mirror

1967

Manual..1

Remote...7

1968

Manual

Round Head......................................2

Rectangular Head.............................3

Remote

Round..8

Rectangular......................................9

1969

Manual..4

Remote...10

1970-1972

Chrome...6

Racing

Drivers...11

Passenger..5

1973-1975

Chrome...6

Racing

Drivers...12

Passenger..5

1976-1981

Chrome...6

Racing

Drivers...12

Passenger..5

Interchange Number: 1
Part Number: 3909197
Type: Manual
Usage: 1967 Firebird, all models and body styles; 1967 Camaro; 1963-67 Chevy II; 1968-72 Nova; 1964-68 Chevelle; 1968 full-size Chevrolet, except coupe.

Interchange Number: 2
Part Number: 9787901
Type: Manual
Usage: 1968 Firebird, all models and body styles; 1968 Tempest.
Notes: Round Head

Interchange Number: 3
Part Number: 3914753
Type: Manual
Usage: 1968 Firebird, all models and body styles; 1968-69 Camaro; 1969 Chevelle; 1969 full-size Chevrolet 1970-72 Chevelle wagon; 1970-72 El Camino.
Notes: Rectangular head

Interchange Number: 4
Part Number: 9782390
Type: Manual
Usage: 1969-70 Firebird, Tempest, LeMans, GTO, full-size Pontiac, Grand Prix all models and body styles.

Interchange Number: 5
Part Number: 9822422 right
Type: Manual
Usage: 1970-1981 Firebird, Grand Prix, LeMans
Notes: Painted racing mirror

Interchange Number: 6
Part Number: 9814436
Type: Manual
Usage: 1970-1981 Firebird, all models and body styles.
Notes: Fits either side chrome

Interchange Number: 7
Part Number: 3899857
Type: Remote
Usage: 1967 Firebird

Interchange Number: 8
Part Number: 9792565
Type: Remote
Usage: 1968 Firebird
Notes: Round head

Interchange Number: 9
 Part Number: 3934583
 Type: Remote
 Usage: 1968 Firebird
 Notes: Rectangular head.

Interchange Number: 10
 Part Number: 9797263
 Type: Remote
 Usage: 1969 Firebird

Interchange Number: 11
 Part Number: 9822423
 Type: Remote
 Usage: 1970 Firebird, Grand Prix, and LeMans.
 Notes: Racing mirror interchange number 12 will fit

Interchange Number: 12
 Part Number: 9865801 left
 Type: Remote
 Usage: 1973-1981 Firebird, Astre; 1970-1981 Camaro; 1974-1977 Monza, Sunbird
 Notes: Racing mirror

Chapter 4: Quarter Panels and Rear End Sheet Metal

Rear Quarter Panels

A used panel must be cut from the car. It is vital that the edges and the panel are solid and free from rust, as weak edges could make the panel fail to hold when it is welded on. Common places for rust on Firebird quarter panels are the bottom area in front and behind the wheel well openings. Also, the process of cutting the panel off can weaken the panel, or damage it. So if you don't know how to do this, it is best to let the professionals at the yard do it.

Used panels are cut at about the middle of the rear panel through the floor panel, middle of the back window, and the rocker panel. This will include the floor pan and the wheel well housing. This cut provides a strong foundation for welding the panel in place.

Though it states that panels are interchangeable from 1970-73, it should be noted that this interchange is a new panel. And there are slight differences in the trunk floor pans in 1970 and 1971-72 and 1973. There is also a difference in the wheel well housings from 1970-71 and 1972-73. Thus, you can't use a used quarter panel from a 1970 Firebird and use it on your 1973 Firebird due to the differences in the trunk floor and the wheel well housings. However, if the panel is cut as a skin there is no problem in the interchange.

1967

Hardtop..1

Convertible...................................2

1968

Hardtop..3

Convertible...................................4

1969

Hardtop..5

Convertible...................................6

1970-73*

All..7

*-Read introduction of this section first

1974

Hardtop..8

1975-1978

All..9

1979-1981

All..10

Interchange Number: 1
   Part Number: 7748126 right 7748127 left
   Usage: 1967 Firebird, hardtop.
   Notes: According to salvage yard owners if only the outer skin is used a Camaro quarter panel will fit.

Interchange Number: 2
   Part Number: 7702812 right 7702813 left
   Usage: 1967 Firebird, convertible.

Interchange Number: 3
   Part Number: 7738876 right 7738877 left
   Usage: 1968 Firebird, hardtop.

Interchange Number: 4
   Part Number: 7741303 right 7741304 left
   Usage: 1968 Firebird, convertible.

Interchange Number: 5
   Part Number: 8784180 right 8784181 left
   Usage: 1969 Firebird, hardtop.

Interchange Number: 6
   Part Number: 7779482 right 7779483 left
   Usage: 1967 Firebird, convertible.

Interchange Number: 7
   Part Number: 9868288 right 9868289 left
   Usage: 1970-73 Firebird, all models.
   Notes: Important see introduction

Interchange Number: 8
　Part Number: 9639543 right 9639544 left
　Usage: 1974 Firebird, all models

Interchange Number: 9
　Part Number: 9676204 right 9676205 left
　Usage: 1975-78 Firebird, all models

Interchange Number: 10
　Part Number: 20160304 right 20160305 left
　Usage: 1979-1981 Firebird, all models

Trunk Lids

Trunk lids are a very sturdy part of the car, and make an excellent buy as a used part. Areas to watch for are damage around the outer lip of the lid; this area is more easily damaged. Another area is just below the latch, this area is the most suitable for rust to appear.

Interchange is without any trim or nameplates and without hinges and a rear spoiler. However, those with a spoiler will have holes drilled in them to mount this device. A deck lid without spoiler can be drilled to accept a spoiler.

Only two deck lids were used. Part number 8783521 was used on the 1967-69 models, and part number 9819030 was used on 1970-1981 models. Both these deck lids can be found also on the Chevrolet Camaro, and will interchange to your Firebird. However, when swapping from Chevrolet to Pontiac some holes may
have to be filled or new ones drilled.

Trunk Lid, Hinges

1967-1968

Hinges..1
Torque rods..................................5

1969

Hinges..1
Torque rods
　Without Spoiler.......................5
　With Spoiler............................6

1970-1981

Hinges..2
Torque rods
　Without Spoiler.......................3
　With Spoiler............................4

Interchange Number: 1
　Part Number: 9709424 right 9709425 left
　Part: Hinges
　Usage: 1967-1969 Firebird, all models and body styles

Interchange Number: 2
　Part Number: 9723492 right 9709493 left
　Part: Hinges
　Usage: 1970-1981 Firebird, all models and body styles

Interchange Number: 3
　Part Number: 9868538 right 9868539 left
　Part: Torque rod
　Usage: 1970-1981 Firebird, all models and body styles. Except with rear spoiler.
　Notes: Left-hand rod is same as interchange 4

Interchange Number: 4
　Part Number: 9868540 right 9868539 left
　Part: Torque rod
　Usage: 1970-1981 Firebird, all models and body styles, with a rear spoiler.
　Notes: Left-hand rod is same as interchange 3

Interchange Number: 5
　Part Number: 7661531 right 7661532 left
　Part: Torque rod
　Usage: 1967-1968 Firebird, all models and body styles; 1969 Firebird without rear spoiler.

Interchange Number: 6
　Part Number: 7733799 right 7870759 left
　Part: Torque rod
　Usage: 1969 Firebird, Camaro all models and body styles, with a rear spoiler.

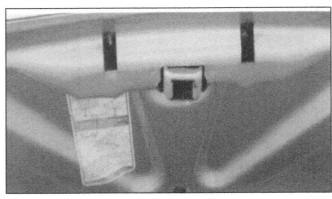
Notice the slots and holes that are required to mount a rear spoiler.

Trunk Floor Pan

1967-1968

All..7

1969

All..6

1970

All..2

1971-1972

All..1

1973

All..3

1974

All..4

1975-1981

All..5

Interchange Number: 1
Part Number: 9836749
Usage: 1971-72 Firebird

Interchange Number: 2
Part Number: 9827172
Usage: 1970 Firebird

Interchange Number: 3
Part Number:
Usage: 1973 Firebird

Interchange Number: 4
Part Number:
Usage: 1974 Firebird

Interchange Number: 5
Part Number: 20123042
Usage: 1975-1981 Firebird

Interchange Number: 6
Part Number: 7779519
Usage: 1969 Firebird, all body styles

Interchange Number: 7
Part Number: 7777341
Usage: 1967-68 Firebird, all body styles

Trunk Lock

1967-1969

All..1

1970

All..2

1971-1972

All..3

1973-1981

All..4

Interchange Number: 1
Part Number: 47553019
Usage: 1967-69 Firebird; 1959-70 full-size Pontiac; 1964-70 Tempest; LeMans; 1969-70 Grand Prix; 1967-69 Camaro. All body styles except wagon.

Interchange Number: 2
Part Number: 9808480
Usage: 1970 Firebird, Camaro

Interchange Number: 3
Part Number: 9849686
Usage: 1971-72 Firebird

Interchange Number: 4
Part Number: 20291279
Usage: 1973-1981 Firebird; 1972-79 Ventura II; 1973-1976 Grand Prix, full-size Pontiac; 1973-76 full-size Oldsmobile, Cutlass all body styles except Station Wagon

Panel, Rear Tail Lamp

1967-1968

All..................................1

1969

All..................................2

1970

All..................................3

1971-1973

All..................................4

1974-1977

All..................................5

1978

All..................................6

1979-1981

All..................................7

Interchange Number: 1
Part Number: 7722988
Usage: 1967-68 Firebird, all body styles.

Interchange Number: 2
Part Number: 8716471
Usage: 1969 Firebird, all body styles.

Interchange Number: 3
Part Number: 9826896
Usage: 1970 Firebird, all models.
Notes: Interchange number 4 will fit

Interchange Number: 4
Part Number: 9869602
Usage: 1971-73 Firebird, all models.

Interchange Number: 5
Part Number: 9736615
Usage: 1974-1977 Firebird, all models.

Interchange Number: 6
Part Number: 20060818
Usage: 1978 Firebird, all models.

Interchange Number: 7
Part Number: 20100540
Usage: 1979-1981 Firebird, all models.

Rear Bumper

1967-1968

All..................................1

1969

All..................................2

1970-1973

All..................................3

1974-1975

Impact Bar..........................5
Fascia..............................4

1976-1978

Impact Bar..5
Fascia...6

1979-1981

Impact Bar..7
Fascia...8

Interchange Number: 1
Part Number: 9788872
Usage: 1967-1968 Firebird

Interchange Number: 2
Part Number: 9795392
Usage: 1969 Firebird

Interchange Number: 3
Part Number: 484947
Usage: 1970-1973 Firebird

Interchange Number: 4
Part Number: 498693
Usage: 1974-1975 Firebird
Notes: Bumper from 1976-78 Firebird fits, but looks visually different.

Interchange Number: 5
Part Number: 549510
Impact bar
Usage: 1974-1978 Firebird

Interchange Number: 6
Part Number: 526899
Outer Fascia
Usage: 1976-1978 Firebird

Interchange Number: 7
Part Number: 10003955
Impact bar
Usage: 1979-1981 Firebird

Interchange Number: 8
Part Number: 10004176
Outer Fascia
Usage: 1979-1981 Firebird

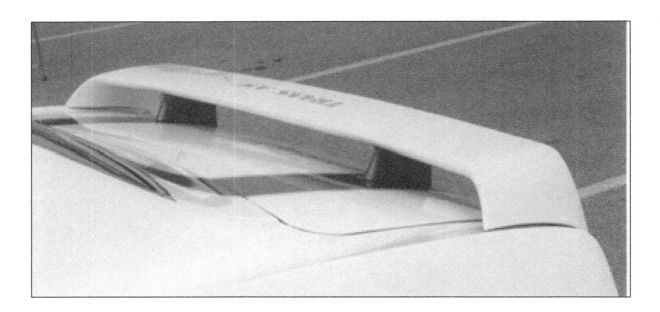

1969 Trans Am Rear Spoiler

Rear Spoilers and Rear Fender Flares

1967-1968

All..2

1969

Except Trans Am..............................2
Trans Am..1

1970-1974

Left Hand..4
Center..3
Right Hand......................................4
Rear fender Flares...........................6

1975

Left Hand..5
Center..3
Right Hand......................................5
Rear fender Flares...........................7

1976-1978

Left Hand..5
Center..3
Right Hand......................................5
Rear Fender Flares..........................7

1979-1981

Left Hand..5
Center..3
Right Hand......................................5
Rear Fender Flares..........................8

Interchange Number: 1
  Part Number: 546530
  Usage: 1969 Trans Am

Interchange Number: 2
  Part Number: 988708
  Usage: 1967-1969 Firebird, except Trans Am; 1967-1969 Camaro

Interchange Number: 3
  Part Number: 480161
  Position: Center
  Usage: 1970-1981 Firebird, 1970-1981 Camaro

Interchange Number: 4
  Part Number: 480159 right 480160 left
  Position: outsides
  Usage: 1970-1974 Firebird

Interchange Number: 5
  Part Number: 493687 right 493688 left
  Position: outsides
  Usage: 1975-1981 Firebird

Interchange Number: 6
  Part Number: 483887 right 48388 left
  Position: Rear Fender Flares
  Usage: 1970-1975 Trans Am

Interchange Number: 7
  Part Number: 526829 right 526830 left
  Position: Rear Fender Flares
  Usage: 1976-1978 Trans Am

Interchange Number: 8
  Part Number: 10006833 right 10006834 left
  Position: Rear Fender Flares
  Usage: 1979-1981 Trans Am

Center spoiler was the same on all 1970-1981 Camaros and Firebirds

Inspect the outer edge carefully for chips and cracks.

Careful inspect fender flares along the mounting points.

Chapter 5: Uni-Body and Roof

Roof Panels

Removing a roof from a salvaged car will require that is cut off the car. This will include the roof plus the front windshield pillars and the back C-pillars. Of course the convertible used a special folding roof frame. This is an assembly that unbolts from the car and is interchanged as a whole.

When inspecting a used roof panel, the number one enemy is rust. On 1967-69 models, a common place where rust forms is the point where roof and quarter panels meet. On the 1970 and later models a common place for rust is at the base of the roofline just below the rear window.

1967-1969

Hardtop..1
Convertible......................................7

1970

Complete panel................................2

1971-72

Complete panel................................3

1973

Complete panel................................4

1974

Complete panel................................5

1975-1981

Complete panel................................6

Interchange Number: 1
Part Number: 785083
Usage: 1967-69 Firebird, hardtop; 1967-69 Camaro hardtop.

Interchange Number: 2
Part Number: 878543
Usage: 1970 Firebird, Camaro.
Notes: Interchange numbers 3, 4 and 5 will fit

Interchange Number: 3
Part Number: 9868294
Usage: 1971-72 Firebird, Camaro.
Notes: Interchange number 4 will fit

Interchange Number: 4
Part Number: 968359
Usage: 1973 Firebird, Camaro.
Notes: Interchange number 5 will fit
 Replacement panel for 1970-73 models

Interchange Number: 5
Part Number: 9739600
Usage: 1974 Firebird, Camaro.

Interchange Number: 6
Part Number: 20088002
Usage: 1975-1981 Firebird, Camaro. Without T-top type roof.
Notes: A roof with t-tops can be fitted to this car.

Interchange Number: 7
Part Number:
Usage: 1967-69 Firebird, convertible; 1967-69 Camaro, convertible.
Notes: Frame

Roofs are highly interchangeable

Convertible Lifts- Hydraulic Cylinders and Mechanical Actuators

1967-1969

Manual..1
Power...2

Interchange Number: 1
Part Number: 4412503
Usage: 1967-1969 Firebird, Camaro; 1964-67 Tempest, Chevelle, Skylark. All with Manual top.

Interchange Number: 2
Part Number: 7704518
Usage: 1967-1969 Firebird, Camaro, with power top.

Rocker Panels

1967

HARDTOP

Inner..2
Outer..1

CONVERTIBLE

Inner..4
Outer..3

1968-1969

HARDTOP

Inner..2
Outer..1

CONVERTIBLE

Inner..4
Outer..5

1970-1973

Inner..8

Outer...6

1974-1981

Inner..8

Outer...7

Interchange Number: 1
Part Number: 7741310 right 7741311
Part: Outer rocker panels
Usage: 1967-69 Firebird hardtop; 1967-69 Camaro hardtop.

Interchange Number: 2
Part Number: 9808988 right 9808989 left
Part: Inner rocker panels
Usage: 1967-69 Firebird hardtop.

Interchange Number: 3
Part Number: 7727648 right 7727649 left
Part: Outer Rock panels
Usage: 1967 Firebird convertible; 1967 Camaro convertible.

Interchange Number: 4
Part Number: 7704362 right 7704363 left
Part: Inner rocker panels
Usage: 1967-69 Firebird convertible; 1967-69 Camaro convertible

Interchange Number: 5
Part Number: 7741314 right 7741315 left
Part: Outer rocker panels
Usage: 1968-69 Firebird convertible; 1968-69 Camaro convertible.

Interchange Number: 6
Part Number: 9818458 right 9818459
Part: Outer rocker panels
Usage: 1970-72 Firebird hardtop
Note: Camaro parts will not fit. Interchange number 7 will fit.

Interchange Number: 7
Part Number: 1680401 right 1680402 left
Part: Outer rocker panels
Usage: 1973-1981 Firebird hardtop.
Notes: Replacement parts for 1970-75 models.

Interchange Number: 8
Part Number: 20202830 right 2020831 left
Part: Inner rocker panels
Usage: 1970-1981 Firebird hardtop.
Notes: Replacement parts for 1970-75 models.

Uni-Body

The interchange here is the car body minus the front end, trunk lid, doors, glass, interior trim and lighting.

You should be aware that this section of the car is considered the frame and is accepted to registration laws of your state so it would be wise to check with your local DMV as each state is different. Note this also applies to you taking a car from the salvage yard putting parts on and titling it as your wrecked Firebird, some states will require you to reregister the car using the main body's serial number. It is always better to ask as many questions as you can and get ALL the answers than it is to go ahead and end with a car with messed up paper work, for you will find that a car with this is essentially only for its parts no matter how rare it is.

UNI-Body Interchange

Model	Interchanges	Model	Interchanges
1967 Hardtop hardtop	1967-68 Firebird	1974	1974 1972, 1974 similar but Roof panel is slightly different.
1967 Convertible	1967 Convertible- 1968 will fit but rocker panels are different	1975	1975-1977 1978 is similar but has different taillight panel
1968 Hardtop hardtop	1967-68 Firebird		
1968 convertible	1968 Convertible- 1967 will fit but rocker panels are different	1976	1975-1977 1978 is similar but has different taillight panel
1969 Hardtop	1969 hardtop 1967-69 Quarter panels different		
1969 Convertible	1969 convertible 1967-69 Quarter panels different	1977	1975-1977 1978 is similar but has different taillight panel
1970	1970	1978	1978
1971	1971-1972	1979	1979-1981
1973	1973 1972, 1974 similar but Roof panel is slightly	1980	1979-1981
		1981	1979-1981

Chapter 6: Glass

General Inspection

Any used glass should be solid and free of cracks and chips. However, modern processes have made it possible to fill some cracks, but only minor surface cracks: To test for a fillable crack, run your thumb nail over the crack on the outside of the glass. If you can feel the crack with your nail, then the crack is unrepairable, and so should be avoided. Also, the glass should be clear, (we're not talking tint here), and not milky looking, which is what happens to cars which have set out in a salvage yard day after day in the temperature extremes.

Before selecting a glass to remove, it might be wise to bring some glass cleaner and paper towels to the yard and clean up the glass; many times the milky look is just dirt and grime. It is wise to sweep the debris off the glass before applying cleaner, to avoid scratching the glass, sight down the glass and look for imperfections and chips, especially along the outer edges of the glass, and next to the firewall.

Windshield

1967-1969

HARDTOP

Clear..1

Tinted..2

CONVERTIBLE

Clear..3

Tinted..4

1970

Without Antenna.

Early

Clear..9

Tinted..10

Late

Clear..11

Tinted..12

With Antenna.

Early

Clear..7

Tinted..8

Late

Clear..5

Tinted..6

1971-1981

Without Antenna

Clear..11

Tinted..12

With Antenna.

Clear..5

Tinted..6

Interchange Number: 1
   Part Number: 7631031
   Type: Clear
   Usage: 1967-69 Firebird, hardtop; 1967-69 Camaro hardtop.

Interchange Number: 2
   Part Number: 7631032
   Type: Tinted
   Usage: 1967-69 Firebird, hardtop; 1967-69 Camaro hardtop.

Interchange Number: 3
   Part Number: 7631033
   Type: Clear
   Usage: 1967-69 Firebird, convertible; 1967-69 Camaro convertible.

Interchange Number: 4
   Part Number: 7631034
   Type: Tinted
   Usage: 1967-69 Firebird, convertible
   1967-69 Camaro convertible.

Interchange Number: 5
   Part Number: 3606235
   Type: Clear
   Usage: Late 1970-1975 Firebird, Camaro with antenna; 1976-77 Firebird, Camaro with bright moldings; 1978-81 Firebird, Camaro.

Interchange Number: 6
   Part Number: 3606236
   Type: Tinted
   Usage: Late 1970-1975 Firebird, Camaro with antenna; 1976-77 Firebird, Camaro with bright moldings; 1978-81 Firebird, Camaro.

Interchange Number: 7
   Part Number: 9870298
   Type: Clear
   Usage: Early 1970 Firebird, Camaro with antenna.
   Notes: Has ball socket mirror

Interchange Number: 8
   Part Number: 9870299
   Type: Tinted
   Usage: Early 1970 Firebird, Camaro with antenna.
   Notes: Has ball socket mirror

Interchange Number: 9
   Part Number: 9870296
   Type: Clear
   ID Tag: W756
   Usage: Early 1970 Firebird, Camaro without antenna.
   Notes: Has ball socket mirror

Interchange Number: 10
   Part Number: 9870297
   Type: Tinted
   ID tag: W755
   Usage: Early 1970 Firebird, Camaro without antenna.
   Notes: Has ball socket mirror

Interchange Number: 11
   Part Number: 3606233
   Type: Clear
   ID Tag: W786
   Usage: Late 1970-1975 Firebird, Camaro without antenna; 1976-77 Firebird, Camaro with bright moldings; 1978-81 Firebird, Camaro.

Interchange Number: 12
   Part Number: 3606234
   Type: Tinted
   ID Tag: W785
   Usage: Late 1970-1975 Firebird, Camaro without antenna; 1976-77 Firebird, Camaro with bright moldings; 1978-81 Firebird, Camaro.

Vent Glass

Vent glass was used only one year in the Firebird-1967. Two different types of glass were used, clear(part numbers 9708666 right and 9708667 left) and tinted (part numbers 9708686 right and 9708687 left).

Interchange is typical of most parts on the early Firebird, meaning that glass from a 1967 Camaro will fit. Also convertible will fit hardtop and vice versa.

Door Glass

1967

Clear..1
Tinted..2

1968-1969

Clear..3
Tinted..4

1970

Clear..5
Tinted..6

1971-1981

Clear..7
Tinted..8

Interchange Number: 1
   Part Number: 7636736 right 7636737 left
   Type: Clear
   Usage: 1967 Firebird, Camaro, all body styles.

Interchange Number: 2
   Part Number: 7636738 right 7636739 left
   Type: Tinted
   Usage: 1967 Firebird, Camaro, all body styles.

Interchange Number: 3
   Part Number: 7777404 right 7777405 left
   Type: Clear
   Usage: 1968-69 Firebird, all body styles.
   Notes: Salvage yard owners say glass from 1968-69 Camaro will fit.

Interchange Number: 4
   Part Number: 7777400 right 7777401 left
   Type: Tinted
   Usage: 1968-69 Firebird, Camaro, all body styles.
   Notes: Salvage yard owners say glass from 1968-69 Camaro will fit.

Interchange Number: 5
   Part Number: 8780303 right 8780304 left
   Type: Clear
   Usage: 1970 Firebird, Camaro, all body styles.

Interchange Number: 5
   Part Number: 8780305 right 8780306 left
   Type: Tinted
   Usage: 1970 Firebird, Camaro, all models.

Interchange Number: 7
   Part Number: 9864176 right 9864177 left
   Type: Clear
   Usage: 1971-1981 Firebird, Camaro, all models.

Interchange Number: 8
   Part Number: 9864178 right 9864179 left
   Type: Tinted
   Usage: 1971-1981 Firebird, Camaro, all models.

Quarter Glass

1967-1969

Clear
Hardtop……………………………….. 1
Convertible…………………………….3

Tinted
Hardtop……………..………………….2
Convertible…………………………….4

Interchange Number: 1
   Part Number: 7707436 right 7707437 left
   Type: Clear
   Usage: 1967-69 Firebird, Camaro. Hardtop only.

Interchange Number: 2
   Part Number: 7707442 right 7707443 left
   Type: Tinted
   Usage: 1967-69 Firebird, Camaro. Hardtop only.

Interchange Number: 3
   Part Number: 7707448 right 7707449 left
   Type: Clear
   Usage: 1967-69 Firebird, Camaro. Convertible only.

Interchange Number: 4
   Part Number: 7707454 right 7707455 left
   Type: Tinted
   Usage: 1967-69 Firebird, Camaro. Convertible only.

Back Glass

1967-1969

Clear……………………………………...1

Tinted………………………………….2

1970-1974

Clear……………………………………3

Tinted

Without Defogger…………………..4

With Defogger……………………….5

1975-1981

Clear..6

Tinted

Without Defogger...............................7

With Defogger....................................8

Interchange Number: 1
Part Number: 76000989
Type: Clear
Usage: 1967-69 Firebird, Camaro, 2-dr. Hardtop.

Interchange Number: 2
Part Number: 7600990
Type: Tinted
Usage: 1967-69 Firebird, Camaro, 2-dr. Hardtop.

Interchange Number: 3
Part Number: 8775901
Type: Clear
Usage: 1970-73 Firebird, Camaro, 2-dr. Hardtop.

Interchange Number 4
Part Number: 8775902
Type: Tinted
Usage: 1970-74 Firebird, Camaro, 2-dr. Hardtop.
Notes: Without defogger grid

Interchange Number 5
Part Number: 8775903
Type: Tinted
Usage: 1970-74 Firebird, Camaro, 2-dr. Hardtop.
Notes: With defogger grid

Interchange Number 6
Part Number: 9733868
Type: Clear
Usage: 1975 Firebird, Camaro, 2-dr. Hardtop; 1976 Firebird, Camaro with bright molding; 1977-81 Firebird, Camaro, all models.

Interchange Number 7
Part Number: 9733869
Type: tinted
Usage: 1975 Firebird, Camaro, 2-dr. Hardtop; 1976 Firebird, Camaro with bright molding; 1977-81 Firebird, Camaro, all models.
Notes: Without defogger grid

Interchange Number 8
Part Number: 20213672
Type: Tinted
Usage: 1975 Firebird, Camaro, 2-dr. Hardtop; 1976 Firebird, Camaro with bright molding; 1977-81 Firebird, Camaro, all models.
Notes: With defogger grid

Chapter 7: Nameplates

General Inspection

Because of the nature of inlayed colors fading, and the bright plating corroding and dulling over time, most nameplates on restored classic automobiles today are bought as reproduction parts. However, there may be instances where the only way to obtain an emblem or nameplate is to purchase it used.

First off, if it is still on the car it would make good sense to first clean the part up. This is done by simply spraying a diluted mixture of cleaner, such as Simple Green® and wipes it off with a soft clean towel. If you do this you can get a much better idea of the condition of the nameplate. Check the inlays; they should be smooth and free of nicks and scratches, if the flat black inlays are faded you can restore them by repainting them. Check the condition of the bright plating; it too should be smooth and free of burrs.

Most emblems were held on with some sort of nut. Those used on later models were held in place by an adhesive. Care must use in removing the latter type, as the best way is applying heat and carefully peeling the emblem back away from the car. Simply removing the nuts and prying or lifting the emblem free more easily removes those that are held on with nuts. However, those on front fenders can pose a problem. If the car is resting on the ground and the fender is damaged or rusted out, but the nameplate is still intact one of the easiest ways to remove the nameplate is to cut the section of the fender around the plate with a torch or cutter. You should always ask if this is permissible, and never take a section out of a good fender this way. If asking for help get one of the crew in the yard to remove it for you. They can use a lift and take it back to the shop, then the last way is to use a hacksaw blade and cut the studs off the nameplate, and then glue it back into place on your car. Note that adhesive is not a proper method of attaching stud type nameplates and it may fail to hold.

You will notice that are interchange section is broken down into individual areas of the car where the emblems are. This was done so as to help you locate the proper emblem. Description of the emblem can be found under the heading identification.

1967-1969 Grille nameplate.

1968 bumper medallion

Emblems, Front Header, Bumper or Grille

1967-1968

Grille

PONTIAC..1

Bumper..5

1969

Grille

PONTIAC..1

Bumper

(400-ci only)....................................14

1970

Grille

PONTIAC..2

Bumper

(400-ci only)....................................15

1971

Grille

PONTIAC..3

350..6

400..7

1972

Grille

PONTIAC..12

350..8

400..9

1973

Grille

PONTIAC..13

350..10

400..11

1974-1975

Grille

PONTIAC..4

Bumper..16

1976

PONTIAC..17
Bumper
Except Special Edition..................16

1977

PONTIAC..17
Bumper
Arrow head....................................18

1978

PONTIAC..20
Bumper
Arrow head
Except Esprit or Trans Am...........19
Esprit...18
Trans Am..18

1979-1981

Arrow head
Except Esprit or Trans Am...........19
Esprit...18
Trans Am..18

1978-1981 Firebird, except Trans Am or Esprit

Interchange Number: 1
  Part Number: 9788859
  Identification: PONTIAC
  Usage: 1967-69 Firebird, all models and body styles.
  Notes: Used on grille.

Interchange Number: 2
  Part Number: 481547
  Identification: PONTIAC
  Usage: 1970 Firebird, all models and body styles.
  Notes: Used on grille.

Interchange Number: 3
  Part Number: 483933
  Identification: PONTIAC
  Usage: 1971 Firebird, all models and body styles, except Trans Am.
  Notes: Used on grille.

Interchange Number: 4
  Part Number: 495108
  Identification: PONTIAC
  Usage: 1974-75 Firebird, all models and body styles.
  Notes: Used on grille.

Interchange Number: 5
  Part Number: 9748667
  Identification: Pontiac crest
  Usage: 1967-68 Firebird with 400-ci V-8; 1967 Grand Prix.

Interchange Number: 6
  Part Number: 483944
  Identification: 350
  Usage: 1971 Firebird, all models and body styles. With 350-ci V-8
  Notes: Used on grille.

Interchange Number: 7
  Part Number: 483945
  Identification: 400
  Usage: 1971 Firebird, all models and body styles. With 400-ci V-8 except Trans Am
  Notes: Used on grille.

Decals are not reusable so no interchange is listed for them

Interchange Number: 8
Part Number: 487706
Identification: 350
Usage: 1972 Firebird, all models and body styles. With 350-ci V-8
Notes: Used on grille.

Interchange Number: 9
Part Number: 487707
Identification: 400
Usage: 1972 Firebird, all models and body styles. With 400-ci V-8 except Trans Am
Notes: Used on grille.

Interchange Number: 10
Part Number: 491119
Identification: 400
Usage: 1973 Firebird, all models and body styles. With 400-ci V-8 except Trans Am; 1973 full-size Pontiac.
Notes: Used on grille.

Interchange Number: 11
Part Number: 491125
Identification: 350
Usage: 1973 Firebird, all models and body styles, with 350-ci V-8.
Notes: Used on grille.

Interchange Number: 12
Part Number: 487732
Identification: PONTIAC
Usage: 1972 Firebird, all models and body styles, except Trans Am.
Notes: Used on grille.

Interchange Number: 13
Part Number: 487735
Identification: PONTIAC
Usage: 1973 Firebird, all models and body styles,
Notes: Used on grille.

Interchange Number: 14
Part Number: 9750025
Identification: Pontiac crest
Usage: 1969 Firebird

Interchange Number: 15
Part Number: 481543
Identification: Pontiac crest
Usage: 1970 Firebird

Interchange Number: 16
Part Number: 494476
Identification: Firebird crest
Usage: 1974-76 Firebird

Interchange Number: 17
Part Number: 498834
Identification: PONTIAC
Usage: 1976-1977 Firebird, on Grille

Interchange Number: 18
Part Number: 499724
Identification: Arrowhead
Usage: 1977 Firebird, Lemans, Ventura II all model; 1978-1981 Firebird except Esprit, Trans Am or S.E. models.

Interchange Number: 19
Part Number: 10003679
Identification: Arrowhead
Usage: 1978-1981 Firebird Esprit, Trans Am or S.E. models.

Interchange Number: 20
Part Number: 549367
Identification: PONTIAC
Usage: 1978 Firebird, on Grille

This emblem was used on all 1967-69 Firebirds with a 400-ci. V-8. A common area to watch on this plate is that the connection bars(arrow) are not broken.

1967 326 hood call out

Hood, Hood Scoop Callouts And Medallions

1967

326-ci	1
400-ci	2
Ornaments	3

1968

350-ci	6
400-ci	2

Ornaments

W/O Ram Air	3
With Ram Air	4

1969

350-ci	6
400-ci	2

Ornaments

EXCEPT TRANS AM

W/O Ram Air	3
With Ram Air	4

TRANS AM

All	5

Interchange Number: 1
   Part Number: 9777848 right 9777849 left
   Identification: 326
   Usage: 1967 Firebird, with 326-ci V-8.

Interchange Number: 2
   Part Number: 9789482 right 9789483 left
   Identification: 400
   Usage: 1967-69 Firebird, with 400-ci V-8.

Interchange Number: 3
   Part Number: 9777957 right 9777958 left
   Identification: Ornaments
   Usage: 1967-68 Firebird, with 400-ci V-8. Without Ram Air; 1969 Firebird with 400-ci V-8 except Ram Air with cable control air inlet.

Interchange Number: 4
   Part Number: 9794283 right 9794284 left
   Identification: Ornaments
   Usage: 1968 Firebird, with 400-ci V-8. With Ram Air; 1969 Firebird with 400-ci V-8 and Ram Air with cable control air inlet.

Interchange Number: 5
   Part Number: 546327 right 546328 left
   Identification: Ornaments
   Usage: 1969 Firebird, Trans Am

Interchange Number: 6
   Part Number: 9792691 right 9792692 left
   Identification: 350
   Usage: 1968-69 Firebird, with 350-ci V-8

1968-1969 350 call out

1967-1969 400 call out

1967-1968 Firebird nameplates and the Firebird Crest, the white inlay is easily restored.

1969 Firebird crest for front fender.

Close up 1967-1968 Firebird crest for front fenders

1969 Firebird nameplate

1970 Firebird front fender nameplate

1977 Firebird nameplate along with Esprit script

1971 Firebird front fender nameplate

1977-1981 Trans Am, Esprit front end medallion.

The Formula nameplate was used by itself from 1971-1975. The 1972-1975 style is shown here. On a very rare 1973 model with the 455 Super Duty. The Firebird emblem part number 1735919 was used on all 1972-1973 Firebirds except Trans Am.

Emblems and Ornaments, Front Fenders

1967-1968

Firebird..9

Crest..1

1969

Firebird..10

Ornaments

Upper..12

Lower..13

1970

Firebird..11

350...2

400...3

Formula 400...4

1971

Firebird..14

Formula 350...5

Formula 400...6

Formula 455...7

Louvers...8

1972

Firebird..14

Crest..15

Formula 350.......................................17

Formula 400.......................................18

Formula 455.......................................19

1973

Firebird..14

Crest..15

Formula 350.......................................17

Formula 400.......................................18

Formula 455.......................................19

1974

Firebird..14

350...16

Formula 350.......................................17

Formula 400.......................................18

Formula 455.......................................19

1975

Firebird..14

Formula 350.......................................17

Formula 400.......................................18

1976

Firebird..14

Formula 350.......................................17

Formula 400.......................................18

Interchange Number: 1
Part Number: 9789589
Identification: Firebird crest
Usage: 1967-68 Firebird, all models and body styles.

Interchange Number: 2
Part Number: 481541
Identification: 350
Usage: 1970 Firebird, with 350-ci V-8.

Interchange Number: 3
Part Number: 480181
Identification: 400
Usage: 1970 Firebird, with 400-ci V-8., except Formula 400.

Interchange Number: 4
Part Number: 481545
Identification: Formula 400
Usage: 1970 Firebird Formula 400.

Interchange Number: 5
Part Number: 483949
Identification: Formula 350
Usage: 1971 Firebird Formula 350

Interchange Number: 6
Part Number: 483948
Identification: Formula 400
Usage: 1971 Firebird Formula 400

Interchange Number: 7
Part Number: 483950
Identification: Formula 455
Usage: 1971 Firebird Formula 455

Interchange Number: 8
  Part Number: 483915 right 483916 left
  Identification: Louvers
  Usage: 1971 Firebird, except Trans Am.

Interchange Number: 9
  Part Number: 9789532
  Identification: Firebird
  Usage: 1967-68 Firebird, all models and body styles.

Interchange Number: 10
  Part Number: 9796319
  Identification: Firebird
  Usage: 1969 Firebird, all models and body styles.

Interchange Number: 11
  Part Number: 481544
  Identification: Firebird
  Usage: 1970 Firebird, all models.

Interchange Number: 12
  Part Number: 9796361 right 9796362 left
  Identification: Ornaments upper
  Usage: 1969 Firebird, all models. Except Trans Am

Interchange Number: 13
  Part Number: 9796363 right 9796364 left
  Identification: Ornaments lower
  Usage: 1969 Firebird, all models. Except Trans Am

Interchange Number: 14
  Part Number: 486904
  Identification: Firebird
  Usage: 1971-75 Firebird, all models. Except Formula or Trans Am

Interchange Number: 15
  Part Number: 1735919
  Identification: Firebird crest
  Usage: 1972-73 Firebird, all models, except Trans Am

Interchange Number: 16
  Part Number: 494564
  Identification: 350
  Usage: 1974 Firebird, with 350-ci V-8

Interchange Number: 17
  Part Number: 487745
  Identification: Formula 350
  Usage: 1972-75 Firebird Formula 350

Interchange Number: 18
  Part Number: 487744
  Identification: Formula 400
  Usage: 1972-75 Firebird Formula 400

Interchange Number: 19
  Part Number: 487746
  Identification: Formula 455
  Usage: 1972-74 Firebird Formula 455

1969 Firebird fender ornaments

1969 Trans Am air scoops

The 1968 Firebird rear quarter panel louvers.

Firebird crest on fuel door of 1968 Firebird.

Shown here is the 1969 lettering and a Firebird crest, which surrounds the trunk lock.

11969 Rear end panel lettering

Lettering 1970 Firebird.

Firebird crest on rear 1970-1981

1969 Firebird rear end callout.

Emblems, Roof and Rear End Panel

1967-1969

400..2

PONTIAC (lettering)...........................4

Crest
1967
Early..11
Late..12
1968..12

1969..7

1970

Esprit..1

PONTIAC (lettering)...........................5

400..3

Crest...10

1971

Esprit..1

PONTIAC (lettering)...........................6

Crest...10

1972-1973

Esprit..1

PONTIAC (lettering)...........................8

Crest...10

1974

Esprit..1

Crest...10

1975-1976

Esprit..1

PONTIAC (Plate)................................9

Crest...10

1977-1978

PONTIAC (Plate)................................9

Crest...10

1979-1981

Crest...10

Interchange Number: 1
Part Number: 9828627
Identification: Esprit
Usage: 1970-75 Firebird Esprit.
Notes: On roof sail panels.

Interchange Number: 2
Part Number: 7728616
Identification: 400
Usage: 1967-69 Firebird, all body styles with 400-ci V-8 except Trans Am.
Notes: On trunk lid

Interchange Number: 3
Part Number: 9808505
Identification: 400
Usage: 1970 Firebird, with 400-ci V-8.
Notes: On trunk lid

Interchange Number: 4
Part Number: See chart for part numbers
Identification: P-O-N-T-I-A-C
Usage: 1967-69 Firebird, all body styles
Notes: Across rear panel

Interchange Number: 5
Part Number: See chart for part numbers
Identification: P-O-N-T-I-A-C
Usage: 1970 Firebird, all body styles
Notes: Across rear panel. 1971 lettering as a whole can replace this interchange.

Interchange Number: 6
Part Number: See chart for part numbers
Identification: P-O-N-T-I-A-C
Usage: 1971 Firebird, all body styles
Notes: Across rear panel. Notes 1972-73 lettering will replace 1970 and 1971 letters as a whole.

Interchange Number: 7
Part Number: 8742310
Identification: Firebird crest
Usage: 1969 Firebird, all body styles
Notes: Rear panel.

Interchange Number: 8
Part Number: See chart for part numbers
Identification: P-O-N-T-I-A-C
Usage: 1972-73 Firebird, all body styles
Notes: Across rear panel.

Interchange Number: 9
Part Number: 1728933
Identification: Pontiac
Usage: 1975-1977 Firebird, all body styles
Notes: Across rear panel.

Interchange Number: 10
Part Number: 20193325
Identification: Firebird medallion
Usage: 1970-1981 Firebird
Notes: On trunk lid

Interchange Number: 11
Part Number: 9789710,
Identification: Firebird medallion
Usage: Early 1967 Firebird
Notes: On rear panel, fuel lid door, used with finger tip lift lid.

Interchange Number: 12
Part Number: 9785962.
Identification: Firebird medallion
Usage: Late 1967-1968 Firebird
Notes: On rear panel, fuel lid door, used with flat lift lid.

Early style lift lid and medallion.

Late 1967 lid and medallion

1967-1969 Firebird Rear End Lettering Chart

Letter	Part Number	Letter	Part Number
P	7712137	I	7712141
O	7712138	A	7712142
N	7712139	C	7712143
T	7712140		

1971 Firebird Rear End Lettering Chart

Letter	Part Number	Letter	Part Number
P	9812717	I	9812721
O	9812718	A	9812722
N	9812719	C	9812723
T	9812720		

1972-73 Firebird Rear End Lettering Chart

Letter	Part Number	Letter	Part Number
P	9855976	I	9855980
O	9855977	A	9855981
N	9855978	C	9855982
T	9855979		

Window trim

Chapter 8: Body Trim

General Inspection

Most of all bright trim work should be just that: bright. Over the years trim will begin to age and the weathering will cause the trim to loss it brightness, and cancerous deposits of rust may form. These examples of trim should be avoided. Select a piece of trim that is solid and free from damage. Limit any damage to scratches in the finish, as this can be repaired with the replating process. However, deep gashes or creases will have to be removed first, and a repaired strip of trim never looks as good as one that has no repair.

Note that some models have dull aluminum or painted trim instead of bright trim. The selection tips listed above still apply; only that brightness of trim is not a selecting point. Body colored or flat black trim can easily be repainted. Dull aluminum trim work should be smooth and free of damage, and is harder to refinish.

Use care in removing trim, as it is during removal or installation that most trim is damaged. If at all possible, use a special tool that is designed for removing trim. This wide mouthed tool allows trim to be removed safely without damage. Or use a wide mouth standard blade screwdriver and work carefully out from the center prying the trim away from its holding clips. Always use care and take your time, speed here will only result in a bent piece of trim and you being unhappy. Note that some trim such as grille and rear end trim may in fact be attached with nuts. Always check first before you attempt to pry the trim off.

Our interchange below is broken down by the trim's location. To find the trim you are looking for first locate the body area, for example: grille trim. Then find that section, look under that heading for your model and note the interchange number and turn to this section to find your interchange number.

Trim, Hood

Moldings are somewhat limited on the hood of the Pontiac Firebird. Its sporty and racy image did not imply to use a lot of chrome. However, a strip of bright work was used along the back edge of the hood on 1970-1975 models. Listed as part number 479085, it was used on all Firebird hoods, due to hood design a molding from a Camaro will not interchange here.

Trim, Windshield

1967

UPPER

Hardtop..2

Convertible

Header...1

Reveal..3

SIDE

Hardtop..7

Convertible.......................................8

LOWER

Hardtop..11

Convertible.....................................12

1968-1969

UPPER

Hardtop..2

Convertible

Header...4

Reveal..3

SIDE

Hardtop..7

Convertible.......................................8

LOWER

Hardtop..11

Convertible..12

1970

Upper..5
Side...9
Lower..13

1971-1972

Upper..5
Side...9
Lower..14

1973-1981

Upper..6
Side...10
Lower..14

Interchange Number: 1
Part Number: 7639786 right 7639786
Location: Upper Header
Usage: 1967 Firebird, Camaro convertible

Interchange Number: 2
Part Number: 7638868
Location: Upper
Usage: 1967-69 Firebird, Camaro hardtop

Interchange Number: 3
Part Number: 7638870
Location: Upper
Usage: 1967-69 Firebird, Camaro convertible

Interchange Number: 4
Part Number: 8714978 right 8714979 left
Location: Upper Header
Usage: 1968-69 Firebird, Camaro convertible

Interchange Number: 5
Part Number: 9808500
Location: Upper
Usage: 1970-72 Firebird, Camaro
Notes: Interchange number 6 will fit.

Interchange Number: 6
Part Number: 9739207
Location: Upper
Usage: 1973-75 Firebird, Camaro; 1976 Firebird, Camaro with bright trim; 1977-81 Firebird, Camaro.

Interchange Number: 7
Part Number: 7639558 right 7639559 left
Location: Side
Usage: 1967-69 Firebird, Camaro hardtop

Interchange Number: 8
Part Number: 7639560 right 7639561 left
Location: Side
Usage: 1967-69 Firebird, Camaro convertible.

Interchange Number: 9
Part Number: 9841148 right 9841149 left
Location: Side
Usage: 1970-72 Firebird, hardtop
Notes: Camaro models use a slight different molding, but will fit.

Interchange Number: 10
Part Number: 9868730 right 9868731 left
Location: Side
Usage: 1973-1981 Firebird, hardtop; 1970-1981 Camaro hardtop.

Interchange Number: 11
Part Number: 7639926 right 7639927 left
Location: Lower
Usage: 1967-69 Firebird, Camaro hardtop

Interchange Number: 12
Part Number: 7648736 right 7648737 left
Location: Lower
Usage: 1967-69 Firebird, Camaro convertible.

Interchange Number: 13
Part Number: 9841146 right 9841147 left
Location: Lower corners
Usage: 1970 Firebird, hardtop
Notes: Camaro molding will not fit.

Interchange Number: 14
Part Number: 3062231 right 3062232 left
Location: Lower corners
Usage: 1971-1981 Firebird, hardtop
Notes: Camaro molding will not fit.

Trim, Front Fenders

1967
Wheel Well......................................1

1968
Wheel Well......................................1

1969
Wheel Well..................................... 2

1970-1975
Wheel Well

Except Trans Am.............................3

Trans Am.........................….....not used

Interchange Number: 1
  Part Number: 9785880 right 9785881 left
  Location: Wheel Well Openings
  Usage: 1967-68 Firebird, all models and body styles; 1967-68 Camaro all models and body styles, except Rally Sport trim.

Interchange Number: 2
  Part Number: 9794773 right 9794774 left
  Location: Wheel Well Openings
  Usage: 1969 Firebird, all models and body styles.
  Notes: Camaro trim will not fit.

Interchange Number: 3
  Part Number: 481536 right 481537 left
  Location: Wheel Well Openings
  Usage: 1970-75 Firebird, all models and body styles, except Trans Am.

Interchange Number: 4
  Part Number: 480641 right 480642 left
  Location: Upper Rear
  Usage: 1970-75 Firebird, all models and body styles.

Trim, Doors

1967-1969
Upper..4

1970
Upper..3

1971-1972
Upper..3

Lower..1

1973-1975
Upper..3

Lower..2

1976-1981
Upper..3

Lower is stick on type

Interchange Number: 1
  Part Number: 8705438 right 8705439 left
  Location: Lower
  Usage: 1971-72 Firebird, all models and body styles.
  Notes: Interchange number 2 will fit. Was replacement part.

Interchange Number: 2
  Part Number: 8705649 (fits either side)
  Location: Lower
  Usage: 1973-75 Firebird, all models and body styles.

Interchange Number: 3
  Part Number: 9815564 right 9815565 left
  Location: Upper decor
  Usage: 1970-1981 Firebird, all models.

Interchange Number: 4
  Part Number: 7737901 right 7737902 left
  Location: Upper reveal
  Usage: 1967-69 Firebird, Camaro with window frame.

Trim, Rocker Panel

1967-1968

All.. 1

1969

All.. 2

1970-1981

.06 wide trim................................ 4

3-inch wide trim............................. 3

Interchange Number: 1
  Part Number: 9785876 right 9785877 left
  Location: Rocker Panel
  Usage: 1967-68 Firebird, all models and body styles, except with Sprint option.

Interchange Number: 2
  Part Number: 9789891 right 9789892 left
  Location: Rocker Panel
  Usage: 1969 Firebird, all models and body styles, Except with Sprint option.

Interchange Number: 3
  Part Number: 481539 right 481540 left
  Location: Rocker Panel
  Usage: 1970-1976 Firebird Esprit; 1970-75 Camaro; 1977 Firebird, except Trans Am; 1979-1981 Firebird, except Trans Am or with deluxe trim.
  Notes: Molding is 3 inches wide

Interchange Number: 4
  Part Number: 481546 (fits either side)
  Location: Rocker Panel
  Usage: 1970-1976 Firebird, all models except Esprit or Trans Am; 1978-1981 Firebird, except Esprit or Trans Am or deluxe trim.
  Notes: Molding is .06 inches wide

Trim, Roof Drip Rails

1967-1969

Roof

Windshield Pillar

Painted... 1

With Vinyl roof.............................. 2

Drip Rails

Without Vinyl roof......................... 3

With vinyl roof............................... 4

1970

Without Vinyl roof......................... 7

With vinyl roof............................... 5

1971

Without Vinyl roof......................... 7

With vinyl roof............................... 8

1972

Without Vinyl roof......................... 7

With vinyl roof

First type.. 7

Second type.................................... 8

1973-1975

Without Vinyl roof......................... 7

With vinyl roof............................... 8

1976-1981

Without Vinyl roof......................... 7

With vinyl roof............................... 9

Interchange Number: 1
   Part Number: 7656807 right 7656808 left
   Location: Windshield pillar
   Usage: 1967-69 Firebird, hardtop
   Notes: Painted moldings

Interchange Number: 2
   Part Number: 7656810 right 7656811 left
   Location: Windshield pillar
   Usage: 1967-69 Firebird, hardtop
   Notes: With Decor or Vinyl top.

Interchange Number: 3
   Part Number: 7637324 right 7637325 left
   Location: Roof, Drip rail
   Usage: 1967-69 Firebird, Camaro hardtop without vinyl roof.

Interchange Number: 4
   Part Number: 7639406 right 7639407 left
   Location: Roof, drip rail
   Usage: 1967-69 Firebird, hardtop with vinyl top.

Interchange Number: 5
   Part Number: 9816514 right 9816515 left
   Location: Roof, Drip rail
   Usage: 1970 Firebird, Camaro with vinyl top or decor package.
   Notes: Interchange number 6 will fit

Interchange Number: 6
   Part Number: 1652948 right 1652949 left
   Location: Roof, Scrap molding
   Usage: 1973-75 Firebird, hardtop with vinyl top

Interchange Number: 7
   Part Number: 9605610 right 9605611 left
   Location: Roof, Scrap molding
   Usage: 1970-1978 Firebird, hardtop without vinyl top; 1970-1976 Camaro with exterior decoration without vinyl top; Early 1972 Firebird, Camaro with vinyl top.

Interchange Number: 8
   Part Number: 9862676 right 9862677 left
   Location: Roof, Scrap molding
   Usage: 1971-1981 Firebird, hardtop with vinyl top; 1971-1981 Camaro with exterior decor package with vinyl roof.
   Notes: Second type only on 1972 models

Interchange Number: 9
   Part Number: 1652948 right 1652949 left
   Location: Roof, Scrap molding
   Usage: 1976-1981 Firebird, hardtop with vinyl top; 1976-1981 Camaro with exterior decor package with vinyl roof.

Trim, Front Extension and Rear Quarter Window

1967-1968

Hardtop... 4

Convertible....................................... 3

1970

Extension...2

1971-1981

Extension.. 1

Interchange Number: 1
   Part Number: 9864182 right 9864183 left
   Location: Extension, behind door glass
   Usage: 1971-81 Firebird, Camaro hardtop with vinyl top or decor group.

Interchange Number: 2
   Part Number: 8809938 right 8809939 left
   Location: Extension, behind door glass
   Usage: 1970 Firebird, Camaro hardtop with vinyl top, or decor group.

Interchange Number: 3
   Part Number: 7743628 right 7743629 left
   Location: Quarter window reveal
   Usage:1967-1968 Firebird, Camaro convertible.

Interchange Number: 4
   Part Number: 7737903 right 7737904 left
   Location: Quarter window reveal
   Usage: 1967- 1968 Firebird, Camaro hardtop with vinyl top, or decor group.

Trim, Rear Quarter Panel

1967

Wheel Well Opening......................... 5

Belt Reveal

Hardtop...1

Convertible......................................2

Louvers

With Black stripe............................. 3

Chrome..3

1968

Wheel Well Opening............................5

Belt Reveal

Hardtop...1

Convertible.......................................2

Louvers..3

1969

Wheel Well Opening............................6

Belt Reveal

Hardtop...1

Convertible.......................................2

1970-1973

Wheel Well Opening............................7

Belt Reveal..4

Front of Wheel Opening........................8

1974

Wheel Well Opening............................7

Belt Reveal..4

Front of Wheel Opening........................9

1975-1981

Wheel Well Opening............................7

Belt Reveal..11

Front of Wheel Opening........................10

Interchange Number: 1
Part Number: 3914078 right 3914077 left
Location: Belt Reveal
Usage: 1967-69 Firebird, Camaro hardtop with vinyl roof or two-tone paint.

Interchange Number: 2
Part Number: 7795005
Location: Louvers
Usage: 1967 Firebird, all models and body styles.
Notes: First type with black stripe.

Interchange Number: 3
Part Number: 4229997
Location: Louvers
Usage: 1967-68 Firebird, all models and body styles.
Notes: Second type chrome.

Interchange Number: 4
Part Number: 9841310 right 9815653 left
Location: Belt Reveal
Usage: 1970-74 Firebird, with vinyl top; 1970

Camaro right hand -side only.
Notes: Paint to match vinyl top.

Interchange Number: 5
Part Number: 4229493 right 4229494 left
Location: Wheel Well Opening
Usage: 1967-68 Firebird, all models and body styles; 1967 Camaro, all models and body styles

Interchange Number: 6
Part Number: 8700967 right 8700969 left
Location: Wheel Well Opening
Usage: 1969 Firebird, Camaro all models and body styles.

Interchange Number: 7
Part Number: 8704037 right 8704038 left
Location: Wheel Well Opening
Usage: 1970-1981 Firebird, all models and body styles;

Interchange Number: 8
Part Number: 8705554 right 8705555 left
Location: Front of Wheel Opening
Usage: 1971-73 Firebird, all models and body styles;

Interchange Number: 9
Part Number: 1154223
Location: Front of Wheel Opening
Usage: 1974 Firebird, all models and body styles;

Interchange Number: 10
Part Number: Varies with color
Location: Front of Wheel Opening
Usage: 1975 Firebird, Grand Prix all models and body styles.
Notes: Adhesive type.

Interchange Number: 11
Part Number: 1659548 right 16595449 left
Location: Belt Reveal
Usage: 1975-1981 Firebird, Camaro with vinyl top

Trim, Rear Window and Rear Roof

1967-1969

Upper...1

Sides..3

Lower...4

1970-1972

Upper...2

Lower/Sides.....................................5

1973-1974

Upper...6

Lower/Side......................................7

1975-1981

Upper...8

Lower/Side......................................9

Interchange Number: 1
  Part Number: 8775869
  Location: Upper
  Usage: 1967-69 Firebird, Camaro hardtop.

Interchange Number: 2
  Part Number: 8798351
  Location: Upper
  Usage: 1970-72 Firebird, Camaro hardtop.

Interchange Number: 3
  Part Number: 8775872 right 8775873 left
  Location: Sides
  Usage: 1967-69 Firebird, Camaro hardtop.

Interchange Number: 4
  Part Number: 7639866 right 8775875 left
  Location: Lower
  Usage: 1967-69 Firebird, hardtop; Right Hand only 1967-69 Camaro hardtop.

Interchange Number: 5
  Part Number: 8799268 right 8799269 left
  Location: Lower and Sides
  Usage: 1970-72 Firebird, Camaro hardtop.

Interchange Number: 6
  Part Number: 9690565
  Location: Upper
  Usage: 1973-74 Firebird, Camaro hardtop.

Interchange Number: 7
  Part Number: 9690566 right 9690567 left
  Location: Lower and Sides
  Usage: 1973-74 Firebird, Camaro hardtop.

Interchange Number: 8
  Part Number: 9738198
  Location: Upper
  Usage: 1975-1981 Firebird, Camaro hardtop.

Interchange Number: 9
  Part Number: 9738210 right 9738211 left
  Location: Lower and Sides
  Usage: 1975-1981 Firebird, Camaro hardtop.

Chapter 9: Interior Hardware

Instrument Panels

The instrument panel, or dash, as it is commonly known, is one of the sturdiest components in the interior of the car. It should be noted that the panel we are discussing in this section is the bare instrument panel. It should be minus all instrumentation and padding, and also the glove box compartment and ashtray. Each of these components can affect the interchange and limits its range.

Because of the nature of the way an instrument panel is mounted, a series of bolts and welds, it is best to leave the removal of the part to the professionals at the yard. Even if you do attempt to remove the panel yourself, bring along a strong helper, as they will be needed.

An important thing to remember when replacing an instrument panel with one that has different accessories than your Firebird originally had, is that it may require you to drill extra holes, or fill holes in the firewall to mount the accessories to accommodate the new panel. This is most common when an in dash tachometer, is installed in a car that originally had no tachometer, a hole is required for the tachometer lead. As for location of this lead consult a restoration guide or part manual.

1967 Firebird used the 1967 Camaro instrument panel.

1967

Upper...*1*

Dash

    Without Air Conditioning................*2*

    With Air Conditioning.....................*3*

    Lower..*4*

1968

Upper...*7*

Dash

Without Air Conditioning..................*5*

With Air Conditioning.....................*6*

Lower..*4*

1969

Upper..*7*

Dash

Without Air conditioning....................*8*

With Air Conditioning.......................*9*

Lower..*4*

1970-1977

Dash...*11*

1978-1981

Dash...*12*

Interchange Number: 1
   Part Number: 7640715
   Location: Upper
   Usage: 1967 Firebird, Camaro all models, body styles and options.

Interchange Number: 2
   Part Number: 7694548
   Location: Dash
   Usage: 1967 Firebird, Camaro all models, body styles and options, except air conditioning

Interchange Number: 3
Part Number: 7694549
Location: Dash
Usage: 1967 Firebird, Camaro all models, body styles with air conditioning

Interchange Number: 4
Part Number: 8726874 right 8726875 left
Location: Lower
Usage: 1967-69 Firebird, all models, body styles and options.

Interchange Number: 5
Part Number: 7726914
Location: Dash
Usage: 1968 Firebird, all models, body styles and options, except air conditioning
Notes: Interchange number 8 will fit, if you use 1969 instrumentation and trim.

Interchange Number: 6
Part Number: 7726915
Location: Dash
Usage: 1968 Firebird, all models, body styles and air conditioning.
Notes: Interchange number 9 will fit, if you use 1969 instrumentation and trim.

Interchange Number: 7
Part Number: 9817107
Location: Upper
Usage: 1968-69 Firebird, Camaro, Nova, all models, body styles and options

Interchange Number: 8
Part Number: 8732344
Location: Dash
Usage: 1969 Firebird, all models, body styles and options, except air conditioning; 1968-69 Camaro, all models and body styles except air conditioning.

Interchange Number: 9
Part Number: 8732345
Location: Dash
Usage: 1969 Firebird, all models, body styles and air conditioning; 1968-69 Camaro, all models and body styles except air conditioning.

Interchange Number: 10
Part Number: 8804044
Location: Dash
Usage: 1970 Firebird, all models, body styles and options, except air conditioning

Interchange Number: 11
Part Number: 496352
Location: Dash
Usage: 1970-1977 Firebird, all models

Interchange Number: 12
Part Number:10018005
Location: Dash
Usage: 1978-1981 Firebird, all models

1970-1981 Firebirds used a one-piece soft foam vinyl covered dash, they can easily be repainted

Panel, Vent Duct

1967-1968

Center

Hardtop

Without Air Conditioning....................1

With Air Conditioning.......................2

Convertible

Without Air Conditioning....................4

With Air Conditioning.......................5

Sides...3

1969

Center

Hardtop

Without Air Conditioning....................6

With Air Conditioning.......................7

Convertible

Without Air Conditioning....................8

With Air Conditioning.......................9

Sides...3

1970-1977

Sides..10

Center

Without Air Conditioning...................11

With Air Conditioning......................12

Upper Dash (1970-1971 only)................13

Sides

Lower...14

Front Duct......................................15

1978-1981

Sides..16

Center

Without Air Conditioning...................17

With Air Conditioning......................18

Interchange Number: 1
Part Number: 7726902
Location: Center
Usage: 1967-1968 Firebird, hardtop except air conditioning.

Interchange Number: 2
Part Number: 7726904
Location: Center
Usage: 1967-1968 Firebird, Camaro hardtop with air conditioning.

Interchange Number: 3
Part Number: 8761930 right 8761931 left
Location: Sides
Usage: 1967-1969 Firebird, Camaro all models, body styles and options.

Interchange Number: 4
Part Number: 7726903
Location: Center
Usage: 1967-1968 Firebird, convertible except air conditioning.

Interchange Number: 5
Part Number: 7726905
Location: Center
Usage: 1967-1968 Firebird, Camaro convertible with air conditioning.

Interchange Number: 6
Part Number: 8745126
Location: Center
Usage: 1969 Firebird, hardtop except air conditioning.

Interchange Number: 7
Part Number: 8745128
Location: Center
Usage: 1969 Firebird, hardtop with air conditioning.

Interchange Number: 8
Part Number: 8745128
Location: Center
Usage: 1969 Firebird, convertible except air conditioning.

Interchange Number: 9
Part Number: 8745127
Location: Center
Usage: 1969 Firebird, convertible with air conditioning.

Interchange Number: 10
Part Number: 9819947 right 9819948 left
Location: Sides
Usage: 1970-1977 Firebird, all models and options.

Interchange Number: 11
Part Number: 9816673
Location: Center
Usage: 1970-1977 Firebird, Camaro all models without
air conditioning.

Interchange Number: 12
Part Number: 9816674
Location: Center
Usage: 1970-1977 Firebird, Camaro all models with air conditioning.

Interchange Number: 13
Part Number: 8792243
Location: Upper dash
Usage: 1970-1971 Firebird, Camaro all models.

Interchange Number: 14
Part Number: 8762091 right 8762092 left
Location: Sides Lower
Usage: 1970-1977 Firebird, all models.

Interchange Number: 15
Part Number: 8782298 right 8782299 left
Location: Front duct, shroud
Usage: 1970-1977 Firebird, all models

Interchange Number: 16
Part Number: 478361 right 478449 left
Location: Sides
Usage: 1978-1981 Firebird, all models and options

Interchange Number: 17
Part Number: 3967970
Location: Center
Usage: 1978-1981 Firebird, Camaro all models without air conditioning.

Interchange Number: 18
Part Number: 3963721
Location: Center
Usage: 1978-1981 Firebird, Camaro all models with air conditioning.

Glove Box, Door and Compartment

1967-1968

Door..1

Compartment

Without A/C......................................9

With A/C..10

1969

Door..2

Without A/C......................................9

With A/C..10

1970

Door

Without A/C......................................3

With A/C..4

Compartment...................................11

1971-1972

Door

Without A/C......................................5

With A/C...6

Compartment...................................11

1973-1981

Door

Without A/C......................................7

With A/C...8

Compartment...................................11

Interchange Number: 1
　Part Number: 9777956
　Part: Door
　Usage: 1967-68 Firebird, all models and body styles.

Interchange Number: 2
　Part Number: 9797557
　Part: Door
　Usage: 1969 Firebird, all models and body styles.

Interchange Number: 3
　Part Number: varies according to color
　Part: Door
　Usage: 1970 Firebird, all models, except with air conditioning.
　Notes: Interchange number 7 will fit.

Interchange Number: 4
　Part Number: varies according to color
　Part: Door
　Usage: 1970 Firebird, all models, with air conditioning.
　Notes: Interchange number 8 will fit.

Interchange Number: 5
　Part Number: varies according to color
　Part: Door
　Usage: 1971-72 Firebird, all models, except with air conditioning.
　Notes: Interchange number 7 will fit.

Interchange Number: 6
　Part Number: varies according to color
　Part: Door
　Usage: 1971-72 Firebird, all models, with air conditioning.
　Notes: Interchange number 8 will fit.

Interchange Number: 7
　Part Number: 100009413
　Part: Door
　Usage: 1973-1981 Firebird, all models, except with air conditioning.
　Notes: Paint to match

Interchange Number: 8
　Part Number: 100009412
　Part: Door
　Usage: 1973-1981 Firebird, all models, with air conditioning.
　Notes: Paint to match

Interchange Number: 9
　Part Number: 3891671
　Part: Compartment
　Usage: 1967-69 Firebird; 1967-68 Camaro all models, except with air conditioning.

Interchange Number: 10
　Part Number: 3891766
　Part: Compartment
　Usage: 1967-69 Firebird,; 1967-68 Camaro all models, with air conditioning.

Interchange Number: 11
　Part Number: 479592
　Part: Compartment
　Usage: 1970-1981 Firebird, all models.

Mirror, Inside Rear View

　A rear view mirror was a standard accessory in the Firebird for all years that are covered in this guide. When selecting a used mirror you should make sure the ball joint that controls the mirror's position is tight and able to hold the mirror in the position you want.

　Adjust the mirror and then holding it by its mounting arm slightly bounce it up and down and note the mirrors reaction, if it changes position, such as drops down, then reject the mirror as the joint is worn out, a very common problem with used mirrors. However, the mirror should not be frozen in one position or so tight that it cannot be easily positioned with one hand. Lastly, check the condition of the mirror glass. It should not be cracked, broken or cloudy. You may have to clean it first to get a good over all look at the unit. Check the condition of the backing; it should be free of damage. Fading is normal and can be repaired by repainting it. Note that the interchange below is without the support and the support itself is a separate interchange.

1967-1968

Mirror..1

Support

Hardtop..7

Convertible..................................8

1967-1968

Mirror..2

Support

Hardtop..7

Convertible..................................8

1970

Mirror

Early..3

Late..4

Support (early models only)

Ball-joint...10

Arms..9

1971-1972

Mirror...4

1973-1981

Mirror...5

Interchange Number: 1
Part Number: 3633013
Part: Mirror Assembly
Usage: 1967-68 Firebird; 1964-68 Tempest; 1961-68 full-size Pontiac; 1967-68 Camaro; 1964-68 Chevelle; 1961-1968 full-size Chevrolet; 1964-67 Chevy II; 1968-early 1970 Nova; 1969 Camaro.

Interchange Number: 2
Part Number: varies with interior color.
Part: Mirror Assembly
Usage: 1969 Firebird, all models and body styles.

Interchange Number: 3
Part Number: 911261
Part: Mirror Assembly
Usage: Early 1970 Firebird
Notes: Support mounted

Interchange Number: 4
Part Number: 917493
Part: Mirror Assembly
Usage: Late 1970-72 Firebird.
Notes: Windshield mount Interchange number 5 will fit.

Interchange Number: 5
Part Number: 911582
Part: Mirror Assembly
Usage: 1973-1981 Firebird; 1976-1979 Ventura II.
Notes: Windshield mount

Interchange Number: 6
Part Number: 91582
Part: Mirror Assembly
Usage: 1973-75 Firebird.
Notes: Windshield mount

Interchange Number: 7
Part Number: 7729476
Part: Support
Usage: 1967-69 Firebird, Camaro hardtop

Interchange Number: 8
Part Number: 9711724
Part: Support
Usage: 1967-69 Firebird, Camaro convertible.

Interchange Number: 9
Part Number: 9816721 right 9816722 left
Part: Support
Usage: Early 1970 Firebird, Camaro
Notes: Long support with arms.

Interchange Number: 10
Part Number: 9825121
Part: Support
Usage: Early 1970 Firebird, Camaro hardtop
Notes: Long support with ball joint

Seat Frames

It is nearly impossible to inspect a seat frame with the upholstery still intact. So it is a better investment to buy a used seat with torn and ripped covers than it is one that has upholstery in good condition. The exception to this rule would be if the covers are in the proper shade and grain for your Firebird.

The best method is to remove the seat covering and the stuffing, this way you can get a true unobstructed view of the condition of the seat springs and the frame itself. The springs should be firm and full, not broken down, which will indicate excessive wear or heavy loads. The frame itself must be intact and not broken. Springs can be replaced, but a broken seat frame should be rejected. Unless the repair is done just right, any altering of the frame will cause the covers not to fit properly.

You should always ask first before removing any cover from the seat, no matter what its condition. If the owner refuses to let you remove the cover, then turn the seat over and carefully inspect the springs from the bottom side. They should be firm and straight, and not gapping away from the bottom of the seat. Place your fingers under the springs and pull up slightly. The springs should have reticence to and bite into your fingers. Springs that you can easily pull down are an indication that they are worn. Next run your fingers and palm along the outer edges of the seat frame, as you press down, feel for any signs of damage, such as a broken frame or unevenness.

Seat backs are even harder to check due to the cover on the back. If you can't remove the cover, first visually check the condition of the cushion back, it should be uniform, and not have any unexplained dips or pockets, which can indicate a broken spring in it.

1967-1968

Bench (1967)..................................21

Passengers....................................11

Drivers...10

Rear Seat

Cushion..19

Back..20

1969

Passengers.....................................9

Drivers..8

Rear Seat

Cushion..17

Back..18

1970

Passengers.....................................7

Drivers..6

Rear Seat

Cushion..15

Back..16

1971-1972

Passengers.....................................4

Drivers..5

Rear Seat

Cushion..15

Back..16

1973-1974

Passengers.....................................1

Drivers..2

Rear Seat

Cushion..12

1975

Passengers.....................................3

Drivers..2

Rear Seat

Cushion..12

Back..13

Interchange Number: 1
Part: Seat -Front Passengers
Usage: 1973-74 Firebird, Camaro; 1973-74 LeMans, Monte Carlo, Chevelle, Skylark, Cutlass.

Interchange Number: 2
Part: Seat -Front Drivers
Usage: 1973-75 Firebird, Camaro; 1973-74 LeMans, Monte Carlo, Chevelle, Skylark, Cutlass.

Interchange Number: 3
Part: Seat -Front Passengers
Usage: 1975 Firebird, Camaro, Nova, Ventura II with bucket seats.

Interchange Number: 4
Part: Seat -Front Passengers
Usage: 1971-72 Firebird, Camaro;
Notes: Seat back frame from 1972 Nova with bucket seats will fit.

Interchange Number: 5
Part: Seat -Front Drivers
Usage: 1971-72 Firebird, Camaro
Notes: Seat back frame from 1972 Nova with bucket seats will fit.

Interchange Number: 6
Part: Seat -Front Drivers
Usage: 1970 Firebird, Camaro

Interchange Number: 7
Part: Seat -Front Passengers
Usage: 1970 Firebird, Camaro

Interchange Number: 8
Part: Seat -Front Drivers
Usage: 1969 Firebird, Camaro

Interchange Number: 9
Part: Seat -Front Passengers
Usage: 1969 Firebird, Camaro

Interchange Number: 10
Part: Seat -Front Drivers
Usage: 1967-68 Firebird, Camaro

Interchange Number: 11
Part: Seat -Front Passengers
Usage: 1967-68 Firebird, Camaro

Interchange Number: 12
Part: Rear Seat Cushion
Usage: 1973-75 Firebird, Camaro

Interchange Number: 13
Part: Rear Seat Back
Usage: 1974-75 Firebird, Camaro

Interchange Number: 14
Part: Rear Seat Cushion
Usage: 1974 Firebird, Camaro

Interchange Number: 15
Part: Rear Seat Cushion
Usage: 1970-72 Firebird, Camaro

Interchange Number: 16
Part: Rear Seat Back
Usage: 1970-72 Firebird, Camaro

Interchange Number: 17
Part: Rear Seat Cushion
Usage: 1969 Firebird, Camaro

Interchange Number: 18
Part: Rear Seat Back
Usage: 1969 Firebird, Camaro

Interchange Number: 19
Part: Rear Seat cushion
Usage: 1967-68 Firebird, Camaro

Interchange Number: 20
Part: Rear Seat Back
Usage: 1967-68 Firebird, Camaro

Interchange Number: 21
Part: Front Bench
Usage: 1967 Firebird, Camaro

Seat Adjustment Rails

1967

Bench Seat......................................1

Buckets

Drivers Seats

Left-hand Side................................3

Right-hand Side..............................2

Passengers Seat

Left-hand Side................................2

Right-hand Side..............................4

1968

Buckets

Driver's Seat

Left-hand Side................................5

Right-hand Side..............................2

Passengers Seat

Left-hand Side................................2

Right-hand Side..............................6

POWER SEATS

Drivers Seat

Left-hand Side................................7

Right-hand Side..............................7

1969

Buckets

Driver's Seat

Left-hand Side.................................5

Right-hand Side..............................2

Passengers Seat

Left-hand Side................................2

Right-hand Side..............................6

POWER SEATS Drivers Seat

Left-hand Side................................8

Right-hand Side..............................8

1970

Buckets

Driver's Seat

Left-hand Side................................9

Right-hand Side.............................11

Passengers Seat

Left-hand Side...............................11

Right-hand Side.............................10

1971-1972

Buckets

Driver's Seat

Left-hand Side...............................12

Right-hand Side.............................13

Passengers Seat

Left-hand Side...............................12

Right-hand Side.............................13

1973-1974

Buckets

Driver's Seat

Left-hand Side...............................15

Right-hand Side.............................14

Passengers Seat

Left-hand Side...............................15

Right-hand Side.............................14

1975-1981

Buckets

Driver's Seat

Left-hand Side...............................16

Right-hand Side.............................18

Passengers Seat

Left-hand Side...............................17

Right-hand Side.............................19

Interchange Number: 1
Part Numbers: 7666873 right 7666874 left
Usage: 1967 Firebird, Camaro with bench seats.

Interchange Number: 2
Part Numbers: 7659752
Usage: Drivers Seat- 1967-69 Firebird, Camaro- right hand side; Passengers Seat- 1967-69 Firebird; 1967-68, Camaro-left-hand side. Except Power seats.

Interchange Number: 3
Part Numbers: 7644518
Usage: Drivers Seat- 1967 Firebird, Camaro -left-hand side.

Interchange Number: 4
Part Numbers: 7644519
Usage: Passenger Seat- 1967 Firebird, Camaro -right-hand side.

Interchange Number: 5
Part Numbers: 8727193
Usage: Drivers Seat- 1968-69 Firebird, Camaro -left-hand side. Except power seats.

Interchange Number: 6
Part Numbers: 7779408
Usage: Passengers Seat- 1968-69 Firebird; 1968 Camaro -right-hand side.

Interchange Number: 7
Part Numbers: 7793545 right 7793546 left
Usage: Drivers Seat- 1968 Firebird with power seats.

Interchange Number: 8
Part Numbers: 8799147 right 8799148 left
Usage: Drivers Seat- 1969 Firebird with power seats.

Interchange Number: 9
Part Numbers: 9809495
Usage: Drivers Seat- 1970 Firebird, Camaro except power seats.

Interchange Number: 10
Part Numbers: 9809494
Usage: Passenger Seat- 1970 Firebird, Camaro except power seats.

Interchange Number: 11
Part Numbers: 9809496
Usage: Drivers Seat- 1970 Firebird, Camaro except power seats- right-hand side; Passenger Seat-1970 Firebird, Camaro except power seats-left-hand side.

Interchange Number: 12
Part Numbers: 9865444
Usage: Drivers Seat- 1971-72 Firebird, Camaro left-hand side; Passenger Seat-1971-72 Firebird, Camaro left-hand side.

Interchange Number: 13
Part Numbers: 9607871
Usage: Drivers Seat- 1971-72 Firebird, Camaro right-hand side; Passenger Seat-1971-72 Firebird, Camaro right-hand side.

Interchange Number: 14
Part Numbers: 1664408
Usage: Drivers Seat- 1973-1981 Firebird, Camaro right-hand side; Passenger Seat-1971-72 Firebird, Camaro right-hand side.

Interchange Number: 15
Part Numbers: 9883756
Usage: Drivers Seat- 1973-1981Firebird, Camaro left-hand side; Passenger Seat-1971-72 Firebird, Camaro left-hand side.

Interchange Number: 16
Part Numbers: 1652301
Usage: Drivers Seat- 1975-1981 Firebird, Camaro left-hand side.

Interchange Number: 17
Part Numbers: 1724574
Usage: Passenger Seat- 1975-1981 Firebird, Camaro left-hand side.

Interchange Number: 18
Part Numbers: 1652303
Usage: Drivers Seat- 1975-1981 Firebird, Camaro right-hand side.

Interchange Number: 19
Part Numbers: 1724571
Usage: Passengers Seat- 1973-1981 Firebird, Camaro right-hand side.

Chapter 10: Interior Trim and Accessories

Crash Pad

Hunting for a good used crash pad, or dash pad, is like a hunt for the Holy Grail, you know it exists but very few have ever seen it. The number one enemy of a dash pad is the most common element in salvage yard- the sun. Brilliant sun blazing down through the glass of a salvaged car will cause the dash to dry out thus the vinyl will split, making it as bad as yours in the first place. However there are cases where the pad is pulled from the car and kept in storage. If it is treated first with oil based spray, like Armor-All ® or even an oil based household dusting spray, the vinyl will not dry out and split.

Basically, the overall condition of the pad is the most important factor to watch for when buying a used dash pad. Other factors are options such as, air conditioned equipped cars used special pads that have provisions for the outlets cut into them. Thus a pad from a non air-conditioned car cannot fit a car with air conditioning or vice versa. Never modify a dash pad, to make it fit the air conditioning outlets, the results are never desirable.

Most dash pads are the simple bolt off design. However, it may require you to be in an upside down position, under the instrument panel to remove it. Note that dash pads were molded in color, but our interchange is not based on color. Instead it centers around the interchange based on the part number for the black colored instrument pad. This was selected because this is one color that was offered each year.

1967

All..1

1968

All..2

1969

All..3

1970-1972

All..4

1973-1977

All..5

1978-1981

All..6

Interchange Number: 1
  Part Number: 7642894
  Usage: 1967 Firebird, Camaro all models, body styles and options.

Interchange Number: 2
  Part Number: 7733950
  Usage: 1968 Firebird, Camaro all models, body styles and options.

Interchange Number: 3
  Part Number: 8748940
  Usage: 1969 Firebird, all models, body styles and options.

Interchange Number: 4
  Part Number: 479401
  Usage: 1970-72 Firebird all models, body styles and options.
  Notes: Interchange number 5 will fit.

Interchange Number: 5
  Part Number: 496352
  Usage: 1973-75 Firebird all models, body styles and options.

Interchange Number: 6
  Part Number: 10018005
  Location: Dash
  Usage: 1978-1981 Firebird, all models

Trim and Nameplates, Instrument Panel

1967

Except Air Conditioning.....................1

Air Conditioning...............................2

Medallion...17

1968

Except Air Conditioning.....................3

Air Conditioning...............................4

Medallion...17

1969

STANDARD TRIM

    Except Air Conditioning.................6

    Air Conditioning...........................5

    Medallion.....................................17

DELUXE TRIM

    Except Air Conditioning.................8

    Air Conditioning...........................7

    Medallion.....................................17

1970-1971

EXCEPT TRANS AM Without Rally Instruments

    Except Air Conditioning.................9

    Air Conditioning...........................11

With Rally Instruments

    Except Air Conditioning...............13

    With Air Conditioning..................14

    Medallion....................................16

TRANS AM

    Except Air Conditioning...............10

    Air Condition...............................12

    Medallion....................................16

1972-1975

EXCEPT TRANS AM Without Rally Instruments

    Except Air Conditioning.................9

    Air Conditioning...........................11

With Rally Instruments

    Except Air Conditioning...............15

    With Air Conditioning..................14

    Medallion....................................16

TRANS AM

    Except Air Conditioning...............10

    Air Conditioning...........................12

1976-1981

EXCEPT TRANS AM Without Rally Instruments

    Except Air Conditioning...............18

    Air Conditioning...........................19

    Esprit 1977-1979 S.E....................27

With Rally Instruments

    Except Air Conditioning...............21

    With Air Conditioning..................22

    Medallion....................................16

TRANS AM

    Except Air Conditioning...............25

Air Conditioning
Except Special edition.........................24
Special Edition
1976..23
1977-1979..26

Interchange Number: 1
  Part Number: 9789353
  Part: Trim plate
  Usage: 1967 Firebird all models, body styles except with air conditioning.

Interchange Number: 2
  Part Number: 9789354
  Part: Trim plate
  Usage: 1967 Firebird all models, body styles with air conditioning.

Interchange Number: 3
Part Number: 9792454
Part: Trim plate
Usage: 1968 Firebird all models, body styles except with air conditioning.

Interchange Number: 4
Part Number: 9792455
Part: Trim plate
Usage: 1968 Firebird all models, body styles with air conditioning.

Interchange Number: 5
Part Number: 9796808
Part: Trim plate
Usage: 1969 Firebird all models, body styles with standard trim and air conditioning.

Interchange Number: 6
Part Number: 9795724
Part: Trim plate
Usage: 1969 Firebird all models, body styles with standard trim without air conditioning.

Interchange Number: 7
Part Number: 9797853
Part: Trim plate
Usage: 1969 Firebird all models, body styles with Deluxe trim and air conditioning.

Interchange Number: 8
Part Number: 9797852
Part: Trim plate
Usage: 1969 Firebird all models, body styles with Deluxe trim without air conditioning.

Interchange Number: 9
Part Number: 478549
Part: Instrument Cluster Panel Trim
Usage: 1970-75 Firebird all models, without air conditioning. Except Trans Am or with Rally instrument cluster.

Interchange Number: 10
Part Number: 481740
Part: Instrument Cluster Panel Trim
Usage: 1970-75 Trans Am without air conditioning.

Interchange Number: 11
Part Number: 481736
Part: Instrument Cluster Panel Trim
Usage: 1970-75 Firebird all models, with air conditioning. Except Trans Am or with Rally instrument cluster.

Interchange Number: 12
Part Number: 481741
Part: Instrument Cluster Panel Trim
Usage: 1970-75 Trans Am with air conditioning.

Interchange Number: 13
Part Number: 481737
Part: Instrument Cluster Panel Trim
Usage: 1970-71 Firebird all models, with Rally instrument cluster without air conditioning. Except Trans Am.
Notes: Interchange number 15 will fit.

Interchange Number: 14
Part Number: 481738
Part: Instrument Cluster Panel Trim
Usage: 1970-75 Firebird all models, with air conditioning and Rally instrument cluster. Except Trans Am.

Interchange Number: 15
Part Number: 489248
Part: Instrument Cluster Panel Trim
Usage: 1972-75 Firebird all models, with Rally instrument cluster without air conditioning. Except Trans Am.

Interchange Number: 16
Part Number: 481542
Part: Firebird medallion
Usage: 1970-1981 Firebird all models.

Interchange Number: 17
Part Number: 9789588
Part: Firebird medallion
Usage: 1967-69 Firebird all models.

Interchange Number: 18
Part Number: 10012499
Part: Instrument Cluster Panel Trim
Usage: 1976-1981 Firebird all models, without air conditioning. Except Trans Am or with Rally instrument cluster.
Notes: Will fit 1970-1975 models.

Interchange Number: 19
Part Number: 10012500
Part: Instrument Cluster Panel Trim
Usage: 1976-1981 Firebird all models, with air conditioning. Except Trans Am or with Rally instrument cluster.
Notes: Will fit 1970-1975 models.

Interchange Number: 20
   Part Number: 10012501
   Part: Instrument Cluster Panel Trim
   Usage: 1976-1981 Firebird all models, with gauges without air conditioning. Except Trans Am.
   Notes: Will fit 1970-1975 models.

Interchange Number: 22
   Part Number: 10012502
   Part: Instrument Cluster Panel Trim
   Usage: 1976-1981 Firebird all models, with gauges with air conditioning. Except Trans Am.
   Notes: Will fit 1970-1975 models.

Interchange Number: 23
   Part Number: 10012507
   Part: Instrument Cluster Panel Trim
   Usage: 1976 Trans Am Special Edition.
   Notes: Gold trim

Interchange Number: 24
   Part Number: 10012503
   Part: Instrument Cluster Panel Trim
   Usage: 1976-1981 Trans Am with air conditioning, except 1976 Special Edition.
   Notes: Bright Aluminum trim

Interchange Number: 25
   Part Number: 10012504
   Part: Instrument Cluster Panel Trim
   Usage: 1976-1981 Trans Am without air conditioning, except Special Edition.
   Notes: Bright Aluminum trim

Interchange Number: 26
   Part Number: 10012505
   Part: Instrument Cluster Panel Trim
   Usage: 1977-1979 Trans Am Special Edition.
   Notes: Gold trim

Interchange Number: 27
   Part Number: 10015647
   Part: Instrument Cluster Panel Trim
   Usage: 1978-1979 Espirt without gauges
   Notes: Gold trim has no holes for gauges, Rare

Trans Am models used a special trim over the instrument panel.

Trim, Radio Panel Cover

1967

With Radio.....................................1

1968

With Radio.....................................2

1969

Without Radio................................3

With Radio.....................................9

1970-1981

Without Radio................................4

With Radio.....................................5

TRANS AM ACC. PLATE

Single..6

Dual..7

Aluminum......................................8

Interchange Number: 1
   Part Number: 9789412
   Usage: 1967 Firebird, all models and body styles. With a Radio

Interchange Number: 2
   Part Number: 9792453
   Usage: 1968 Firebird, all models and body styles. With a Radio

Interchange Number: 3
   Part Number: 9796880
   Usage: 1969 Firebird, all models and body styles. Without a Radio

Interchange Number: 4
   Part Number: 479381
   Usage: 1970-1981 Firebird, all models and body styles. Without radio.

Interchange Number: 5
   Part Number: 478997
   Usage: 1970-1981 Firebird, all models and body styles. With a radio.

Interchange Number: 6
   Part Number: 481742
   Usage: 1970-1981 Trans Am. Single accessory plate trim.

Interchange Number: 7
   Part Number: 481744
   Usage: 1970-1981 Trans Am. dual accessory plate trim.

Interchange Number: 8
   Part Number: 480856
   Usage: 1970-1981 Trans Am. Aluminum accessories plate trim.

Interchange Number: 9
   Part Number:
   Usage: 1969 Firebird with radio.

Door Panels And Quarter Panels

Used door panels can be a wise buy. When buying a used panel, color is not a concern, as the panel can be repainted to match your trim. Check the panel and make sure it is not warped, natural weather of a panel will cause the panel to draw up in the middle, and this is especially true of panels that have already been removed. If the panel will not lay flat, it will not fit your door properly and the clips will not hold it in place.

Speaking of clips, turn the panel over and make sure that the clip support areas in the panel are strong and not damaged. A broken clip support will not allow you to properly insert the holding clips in the back of the door panel. Also check the back of the panel to be sure it is free of mold. On the front of the panel check the condition of the vinyl and the trim, all trim should be mounted securely and not be loose. Also, before you start looking make a note, if your car came with standard or deluxe interior trim, as many times different door panels were used with the Deluxe trim and standard trim panel will not work.

Inspection is the same with quarter panel trim pads, as it is with door panels. However, while there are no body style restrictions for the door panels, a convertible and hardtop used the same panel, there are restrictions on body styles with quarter panels. Convertible models used special quarter panel trim pads, and other body styles will not fit.

As for an interchange range 1967-1969 models differ each year and are not interchangeable with each other. For the 1972-1981 models there is a little interchanging available, the lower panel was the same. However, the upper panels were different each year.

Arm Rest, Front

There is a great interchange range available here. For the trim on 1968-1969 models, it can be found on any 1968-2969 Pontiac model, except LeMans 4-door hardtop, Tempest wagon or convertible or Bonneville or Grand Prix.

The base part number 4493308 was used in 1967 Firebirds and has no interchange. Part numbers 7755978 right-hand and 7755979 left-hand were used in 1968 Firebirds, but can also be found in 1968 Tempest, LeMans, and GTO along with Catalina and Executive models, except wagons. For 1969 the part numbers were changed to 8769926 right and 8769927 left, and was used in all 1969 Tempest, LeMans, GTO along Catalina and Executive models except wagons. It will not fit earlier models.

An armrest pad part number 9814916 was used on all 1970-71 Firebirds. While from 1972-75 it is listed as part number 9600968. Above part numbers are for black color only, you will have to repaint armrests to match your trim.

Trim and Nameplates, Door Panel

1967

STANDARD TRIM

Upper..1

Lower...2

CUSTOM TRIM

Upper..3

Lower...4

Firebird...12

1968-1969

Upper

Without Remote Control Mirror..........5

With Remote Control Mirror

Front..6

Rear...7

Lower...8

Medallion......................................10

Firebird (1968)..............................12

Door Pull.......................................11

1970-1972

Door Pull...9

1973-1975

Door Pull.......................................13

Firebird...14

Interchange Number: 1

Part Number: 7639888 (either side) Part: Upper Molding
Usage: 1967 Firebird, all models and body styles with standard interior trim.

Interchange Number: 2

Part Number: 4467508 (either side) Part: Lower Molding
Usage: 1967 Firebird, all models and body styles with standard interior trim.

Interchange Number: 3

Part Number: 7669268 (either side) Part: Upper Molding
Usage: 1967 Firebird, all models and body styles with custom interior trim.

Interchange Number: 4

Part Number: 7669267 (either side) Part: Lower Molding
Usage: 1967 Firebird, all models and body styles with custom interior trim.

Interchange Number: 5

Part Number: 7737762
Part: Upper Molding
Usage: 1968-69 Firebird, all models and body styles without remote control mirror; 1968-69 Firebird passenger side with standard trim.

Interchange Number: 6

Part Number: 7726724
Part: Upper Front Molding
Usage: 1968-69 Firebird, all models and body styles with remote control mirror.

Interchange Number: 7

Part Number: 7759450
Part: Upper Rear Molding
Usage: 1968-69 Firebird, all models and body styles with remote control mirror.

Interchange Number: 8
Part Number: 7743242
Part: Lower Molding
Usage: 1968 Firebird, all models and body styles with standard trim; 1969 Firebird all models and body styles with custom trim.

Interchange Number: 9
Part Number: varies with color
Part: Pull strap
Usage: 1970-71 Firebird, all models

Interchange Number: 10
Part Number: 7771090
Part: Medallion
Usage: 1968-69 Firebird, all models and body styles

Interchange Number: 11
Part Number: varies with color
Part: Door Pull
Usage: 1968-69 Firebird, all models and body styles

Interchange Number: 12
Part Number: 7728725
Part: Firebird
Usage: 1967-68 Firebird, all models and body styles

Interchange Number: 13
Part Number: varies with color
Part: Door Pull
Usage: 1973-75 Firebird, all models and body styles
Notes: A few early 1973 Firebirds had Interchange number 9 style.

Interchange Number: 14
Part Number: 1653525
Part: Firebird
Usage: 1975 Firebird, all models and body styles

Console

A used console is an excellent buy and with a little prep work and repainting a used console can look as good as a reproduction unit, and for less than half the cost.

First, know that of all later versions, the 1970-1975 models of the Firebirds, the console is based on the transmission type platform, meaning that a console from a manual equipped car will not fit a car with an automatic transmission, or vise versa.

Check the overall condition of the base, it is made of hard molded plastic, and plastic can break or crack under stress. Areas to watch are the point where shifter and console meet, and compartment area. Also check the condition of the door, often this unit is abused and the hinges get broken or bent and the door will not open and close properly, so open and close it a few times to make sure it works properly. A even more common problem to the 1970-1975 console is the forward end of it, and the map pocket. Many times this area was cut up or drilled into, to mount an auxiliary radio or tape player. Also check along the outer edges of the base, where it meets with the floor. Scuffs and cracks are common here also.

The base you select should be solid and free of damage or cracks. Light scuffmarks or discolorations are okay, as long as they don't damage the grain of the plastic. Even though the bases were molded in a color that was keyed to the interior trim, color is not a concern as it can be easily repainted.

1967

Manual Trans..................................1

Automatic Trans............................1

1968-1969

Manual Trans..................................2

Automatic Trans............................2

1970

Manual Trans..................................3

Automatic Trans............................4

1971

Manual Trans.

Front..5

Rear...7

Automatic Trans................................4

1972-1975

Manual Trans.

Front..5

Rear...7

Automatic Trans.

Front..6

Rear...7

1976-1979

Manual Trans...................................8
Automatic..9

1980

Manual Trans...................................10
Automatic..11

1981

Manual Trans...................................12
Automatic..14

Interchange Number: 1
Part Number: 3918725
Transmission: All
Usage: 1967 Firebird, all models and body styles; 1967 Camaro, with floor shift and no gauge package.

Interchange Number: 2
Part Number: 9793278
Transmission: All
Usage: 1968-69 Firebird, all models and body styles.

Interchange Number: 3
Part Number: 480104
Transmission: Manual
Usage: 1970 Firebird, all models and body styles.

Interchange Number: 4
Part Number: 479536
Transmission: Automatic
Usage: 1970-71 Firebird, all models and body styles.

Interchange Number: 5
Part Number: 482792-Front
Transmission: Manual
Usage: 1971-75 Firebird, all models and body styles.

Interchange Number: 6
Part Number: 482797-Front
Transmission: Automatic
Usage: 1972-75 Firebird, all models and body styles.

Interchange Number: 7
Part Number: 9790585-Rear
Transmission: All
Usage: 1971-75 Firebird, all models and body styles.

Interchange Number: 8
Part Number: 10009289
Transmission: Manual
Usage: 1976-1979 Firebird, all models and body styles

Interchange Number: 9
Part Number: 10009290
Transmission: Automatic
Usage: 1976-1979 Firebird, all models and body styles

Interchange Number: 10
Part Number: 100011164
Transmission: Manual
Usage: 1980 Firebird, all models and body styles

Interchange Number: 11
Part Number: 100011163
Transmission: Automatic
Usage: 1980 Firebird, all models and body styles

Interchange Number: 12
Part Number: 100013238
Transmission: Manual
Usage: 1980 Firebird, all models and body styles

Interchange Number: 14
Part Number: 100053952
Transmission: Automatic
Usage: 1980 Firebird, all models and body styles

Rear Shelf Panel

Without a doubt this is the most abused item in the interior of a Firebird. Very few survived the incautious surgery of installing a stereo in the 1970's. Too many would-be back yard installers, this author included, cut the holes in the rear shelf panel to make way for huge 60 oz. speakers.

If you find a panel that has survived this fate, your next check should be for damage from the weather elements. The blazing sun can dry out a panel and warp it, making it unusable. A good way to check for this is to visually sight down it for unexplained contours or bends. Also, rub your palm along the surface; it should feel smooth. A rough dried out feel is a sure sign that the fiberboard is unusable. Note that finding a rear shelf panel in good condition in the salvage yard is rare. But it can be done, and the good news is color doesn't matter because it can be easily repainted.

1967-1968

All..1

1969

All..2

1970

Without Speaker...............................3

With Speaker....................................4

1971-1974

Without Speaker...............................5

With Speaker....................................6

1975-1981

Without Speaker...............................7

With Speaker....................................8

Interchange Number: 1
Part Number: Varies with color
Usage: 1967-68 Firebird, Camaro hardtop.

Interchange Number: 2
Part Number: Varies with color
Usage: 1969 Firebird, Camaro hardtop.

Interchange Number: 3
Part Number: Varies with color
Usage: 1970 Firebird, Camaro hardtop, without speaker provision.
Notes: Interchange Number 4 will fit but has provision of speakers.

Interchange Number: 4
Part Number: Varies with color
Usage: 1970 Firebird, Camaro hardtop.
With speaker provision

Interchange Number: 5
Part Number: Varies with color
Usage: 1971-1973 Firebird, Camaro hardtop. Without speaker provision
Notes: Interchange Number 6 will fit but has provision of speakers.

Interchange Number: 6
Part Number: Varies with color
Usage: 1971-1974 Firebird, Camaro hardtop.
With speaker provision

Interchange Number: 7
Part Number: Varies with color
Usage: 1975-1981 Firebird, Camaro hardtop. Without speaker provision
Notes: Interchange Number 8 will fit but has provision of speakers.

Interchange Number: 8
Part Number: Varies with color
Usage: 1975-1981 Firebird, Camaro hardtop, with speaker provision.

SUPER INTERCHANGE NOTE:
All 1970-1974 panels will interchange; there is just a difference in the texture. 1975 and later style will not fit earlier models due to a difference in the length of the panel.

Seat Belts and Shoulder Straps

These units are an excellent buy as a used part, they may not have the clean neat look of reproduction belts, but in most cases used is the only way you can get the belt you want. The good news is that they are sturdy parts and take the everyday abuse that is dished out during their life. Also belts, especially later models, are a GM part that can be found in a variety of models.

When selecting belts look at the webbing: it should be free of cuts and frays, the buckle should be clean and free of scratches and complete. A common problem is that the center logo button will be missing. With the belts in good shape, next buckle them together and see if they work properly. They should buckle easily. Try to pull the belts apart when they are buckled together, they should remain buckled and not pull apart. Reject any belt that doesn't. Next the belts should also unbuckle with just a touch of the release button. Any belt that that takes more than one touch should be rejected.

Belts are easily identifiable by the part number that is printed on a patch on the underside of each set of belts. Our interchange below is not based on color but instead the basic belt design that was installed in your car.

There are two types belts- those with the standard trim which usually have colored – key buckles and those with the Deluxe trim which usually has brushed aluminum buckles, these sets can be interchanged if swapped together and all belts are swapped out. Physical fit belts are all 1967-1969 lap belts will fit, all 1970-1981 belts will swap with each other, however to keep the right belt there are very few interchanges between model years.

The 1967-1968 standard belts are the same, but the custom belts are different each year. The 1971-1972 Standard belts are again the same, but the custom belts are not. Note there was switch over in belt design in 1972 models; the early model used a four point hitch design and the latter used a three-point design. The two are not interchangeable with each other, unless both the buckle and hitch are interchanged together.

Belts were again changed in the middle of the 1974 model year. The letter appears on the underside of the first type with a black wire, while the second type has the letter X on the bottom of the buckle and has a gray wire. There is no difference in the way the belts fit, so either can fit. Note that Camaro belts are the same and will fit your Firebird.

Lap belts have a great span of interchangeability especially in the first generation models. The 1967 Firebirds used the same rear seat belts that were used in the Camaro, and also the Chevelle, Tempest, Cutlass, Chevy II, and all full-size Chevrolet, Oldsmobile, and Buicks, along with the full-size Pontiac. Just make sure they are from the rear seat. This also applies to the shoulder straps.

The 1968-1969 models used the same seats in the seat belts both years, and were used on the same models listed above but were the 1968 and 1969 models. The other lap belts were changed every year. Again physical fit is all 1970-1981 models will fit any of the second generation birds.

Standard Firebird Instrumentation.

Chapter 11: Electrical Accessories

EXTERIOR COMPONENTS

Lamp Assemblies

The first thing you should watch for when selecting used lamps is the condition of the lens. It should be bright and not cracked or broken. Uneven temperatures and bright sunlight can cause the colored plastic to fade and discolor. To get an accurate inspection of the lens, it is best to clean it off first with a clean soft cloth and a mild cleanser.

Even if the lens is in good shape, then you should remove it, and if possible, inspect the lamp housing. Viewing the lamp assemblies from the trunk you can sometimes do this. All housings should be solid and free of damage. Discoloration should not be a big concern here as they can be easily repainted and made to appear brand new.

FRONT TURN LAMPS

1967

All..1

1968

Early..2

Late...3

1969

All..9

1970-1971

Lamp..4
Bezels..12

1972

Clear Lens

Separate..4

Part of Harness................................5

Amber Lens

Lens...6
Bezels..12

1973

Lamp..6
Bezels..12

1974

Lamp..7
Bezels..12

1975

Lamp..8
Bezels..12

1976

Lamp..10
Bezels..11

1977-1978

Lamp..10
Bezels..11

1979-1981

Lamp..10
Bezels..14

Interchange Number: 1
  Part Number: 916534 right 916533 left
  Part: Front Turn Lamp
  Usage: 1967 Firebird all models, body styles and options.

Interchange Number: 2
  Part Number: 916616 right 916617 left
  Part: Front Turn Lamp
  Usage: Early 1968 Firebird all models, body styles and options.
  Notes: Two-bulb design

Interchange Number: 3
Part Number: 916910 right 916911 left
Part: Front Turn Lamp
Usage: Late 1968 Firebird all models, body styles and options.
Notes: Single bulb design can fit Interchange number two, just cut off the unused brown colored wire. Note, this could cost you points at a show.

Interchange Number: 4
Part Number: 916814 either side
Part: Front Turn Lamp
Usage: 1970-72 Firebird all models.
Notes: Separate Clear lens

Interchange Number: 5
Part Number: 5963966 either side
Part: Front Turn Lamp
Usage: 1972 Firebird all models with bulb part of harness type with clear lens.

Interchange Number: 6
Part Number: 5965930 either side
Part: Front Turn Lamp
Usage: 1972-73 Firebird all models with bulb part of harness type with amber lens.

Interchange Number: 7
Part Number: 912166 right 912165 left
Part: Front Turn Lamp
Usage: 1974 Firebird, Ventura II all models, and body styles, except GTO.

Interchange Number: 8
Part Number: 917400 right 917399 left
Part: Front Turn Lamp
Usage: 1975 Firebird all models.
Note: will fit 1970-1974 models

Interchange Number: 9
Part Number: 916814 either side
Part: Front Turn Lamp
Usage: 1969 Firebird, all models and body styles.

Interchange Number: 10
Part Number: 912992 right 912991 left
Part: Front Turn Lamp
Usage: 1976 Firebird all models.

Interchange Number: 11
Part Number: 499855 right 499856 left
Part: Bezels, Front turn lamps
Usage: 1976-1978 Firebird all models.

Interchange Number: 10
Part Number: 913648 right 913647 left
Part: Front Turn Lamp
Usage: 1977-1978 Firebird all models.

Interchange Number: 12
Part Number: 479083 right 479084 left
Part: Bezels, Front turn lamps
Usage: 1970-1975 Firebird all models.

Interchange Number: 13
Part Number: 914010 right 914009 left
Part: Front Turn Lamp
Usage: 1979-1981 Firebird all models.

Interchange Number: 14
Part Number: 914010 right 914009 left
Part: Front Turn Lamp
Usage: 1979-1981 Firebird all models.

1968 Firebird lamp

1969 Front turn lamp

1970-early 1972 front lamps have a clear lens.

SIDE LAMPS, FRONT FENDER AND REAR QUARTER PANELS

1967

Not Used

1968

Front

Part of front assembly

Rear……………………………………….5

1969

Front……………………………………..1

Rear……………………………………….3

1970-1981

Front
Lamp……………………………………...6
Bezel……………………………………..7
Rear……………………………………….4

Interchange Number: 1
Part Number: 911138 either side
Part: Side Lamp, Front Fender
Usage: 1969 Firebird, Tempest all models, and body styles.

Interchange Number: 2
Part Number: 917400 right 917399 left
Part: Side Lamp, Front Fender
Usage: 1970-1978 Firebird all models.

Interchange Number: 3
Part Number: 911139 either side
Part: Side Lamp, Rear Quarter
Usage: 1969 Firebird, all models and body styles.

Interchange Number: 4
Part Number: 917402 right 917401 left
Part: Side Lamp, Rear Quarter
Usage: 1970-1981 Firebird all models.

Interchange Number: 5
Part Number: 5960470-Housing 5960473-lens
Part: Side Lamp, Rear Quarter
Usage: 1968 Firebird, all models and body styles.

Interchange Number: 6
Part Number: 9479083 right 9479084 left
Part: Bezel, Side Lamp Front Fender
Usage: 1970-1981 Firebird all models.

TAIL LAMPS

1967-1968

Housing…………………………………..2
Lens……………………………………....1

1969

Housing…………………………………..3
Lens……………………………………....4

1970-1972

Housing…………………………………..6
Lens…………………………………….... 5

1973

Housing..6
Lens..7

1974-1975

Housing..9
Lens..8

1976-1978

Housing..9
Lens
Except Trans Am...................................8
Trans Am..10

1979-1979

Without Custom Exterior Group
Housing..11
Lens..15
With Custom Exterior Group
Housing..12
Lens
Inner
Main...14
Back up..13
Outer..16

1980

Without Custom Exterior Group
Housing..11
Lens..15
With Custom Exterior Group
Housing..12
Lens
Except Esprit
Inner
Main...14
Back up..13
Outer..16
Esprit..17

Interchange Number: 1
Part Number: 5959716 either side
Part: Tail Lamp, Lens
Usage: 1967-68 Firebird, all models and body styles.

Interchange Number: 2
Part Number: 59559712 either side
Part: Tail Lamp, Housing
Usage: 1967-68 Firebird, all models and body styles.

Interchange Number: 3
Part Number: 596210 right 596211 left
Part: Tail Lamp, Housing
Usage: 1969 Firebird, all models and body styles.

Interchange Number: 4
Part Number: 5961294 either side
Part: Tail Lamp, Lens
Usage: 1969 Firebird, all models and body styles.

Interchange Number: 5
Part Number: 5962936 right 5962935 left
Part: Tail Lamp, Lens
Usage: 1970-1971 Firebird all models.

Interchange Number: 6
Part Number: 5963088 right 5963089 left
Part: Tail Lamp, Housing
Usage: 1970-1973 Firebird all models.

Interchange Number: 7
Part Number: 5964664 right 5964663 left
Part: Tail Lamp, Lens
Usage: 1973 Firebird all models.
Notes: will fit 1970-1972 models.

Interchange Number: 8
Part Number: 5949828 right 5949829 left
Part: Tail Lamp, Lens
Usage: 1974-1975 Firebird, all models; 1976-1978 Firebird, all models except Trans Am

Interchange Number: 9
Part Number: 5968978 right 5968977 left
Part: Tail Lamp, Housing
Usage: 1974-1976 Firebird all models.

Interchange Number: 10
Part Number: 5949847 right 5949848 left
Part: Tail Lamp, Lens
Usage: 1976-1978 Trans Am

Interchange Number: 11
Part Number: 5970714 right 5970713 left
Part: Tail Lamp, Housing
Usage: 1979-1981 Firebird all models, except with custom exterior group.

Interchange Number: 12
Part Number: 5970794 right 5970793 left
Part: Tail Lamp, Housing
Usage: 1979-1981 Firebird with custom exterior group.
Notes: Has extra inner lens.

Interchange Number: 13
>Part Number: 5970808 right 5970807 left
>Part: Tail Lamp, Lens
>Usage: 1979-1981 Firebird, with custom exterior group
>Notes: Extra inner lens

Interchange Number: 14
>Part Number: 5970806 right 5970805 left
>Part: Tail Lamp, Lens
>Usage: 1979-1981 Firebird, with custom exterior group
>Notes: Inner lens

Interchange Number: 15
>Part Number: 5970720 right 5970719 left
>Part: Tail Lamp, Lens
>Usage: 1979-1981 Firebird, all models except with custom exterior group or 1980 Esprit
>Notes: Main outer lens.

Interchange Number: 16
>Part Number: 5937036 right 5937035 left
>Part: Tail Lamp, Lens
>Usage: 1979-1981 Firebird, all models with custom exterior group except 1980 Esprit
>Notes: Main outer lens with reflex

Interchange Number: 17
>Part Number: 5937874 right 5937873 left
>Part: Tail Lamp, Lens
>Usage: 1980 Esprit

1968 rear marker

1969 rear marker was very unique

1969 front side lamp was very simple

1969 tail lamps

LICENSE PLATE LAMPS

1967-1968

All...1

1969

All...2

1970-1972

All...3

1973

All...4

1974-1978

All...5

1979-1981

All...6

Interchange Number: 1
 Part Number: 916634
 Usage: 1967-68 Firebird, all models and body styles.

Interchange Number: 2
 Part Number: 910386
 Usage: 1969 Firebird, all models and body styles.

Interchange Number: 3
 Part Number: 911220
 Usage: 1970-1971 Firebird all models.
 Notes: Interchange number 3 is said to fit

Interchange Number: 4
 Part Number: 917647
 Usage: 1973 Firebird all models; 1969-1972 Grand Prix; 1971-1972 full-size Pontiac, all models except wagon

Interchange Number: 5
 Part Number: 928790
 Usage: 1974-1978 Firebird all models.

Interchange Number: 6
 Part Number: 912116
 Usage: 1979-1981 Firebird all models.

1970-1973 tail lamp.

Difference in 1979-1981 tail lamps above is with exterior group, below is without it.

Headlamp Bezels, Headlamp Rings and Housings

1967-1969

Inboard

Right-hand.....................................1

Left-hand.......................................2

Outboard

Right-hand.....................................3

Left-hand.......................................4

Bezels 1969 only

 Inner..7

 Outer...8

1970-1973

Rings...5

Bezels..9

1974-1976

Rings...6

Bezels..10

1977-1978

Housing
Outer lamps..................................11
Inner lamps..................................12

Rings...13

1979-1981

Housing
Outer lamps..................................11
Inner lamps..................................12

Rings...13
Bezels
Base Firebird................................14
Trans Am......................................15
Formula..15
Esprit..15

Interchange Number: 1
  Part Number: 5950506- right
  Part: Headlamp Ring-Inboard
  Usage: 1967-69 Firebird all models; 1963-64 full-size
   Pontiac (lower headlamp); 1970-72 Tempest, full-size Pontiac (inner headlamp type 1); 1970 Grand Prix (left-hand inner lamp); 1973-74 full-size Pontiac.

Interchange Number: 2
  Part Number: 5950500- left
  Part: Headlamp Ring-Inboard
  Usage: 1967-69 Firebird all models; 1965-66 full-size Pontiac (lower headlamp); 1965-68 Tempest, all models (lower or inner headlamp); 1968 full-size Pontiac (inner headlamp) 1969 Tempest, full-size Pontiac (inner left-hand headlamp type 1); 1970 Grand Prix (right-hand inner
   lamp); 1973-74 full-size Pontiac (left-hand inner)

Interchange Number: 3
  Part Number: 5950513- right
  Part: Headlamp Ring-Outboard
  Usage: 1967-69 Firebird all models; 1970-72 full-size Pontiac, Tempest (outer right-hand headlamp); 1970 Grand Prix (stamped "C" on tab); 1973-74 full-size Pontiac.

Interchange Number: 4
  Part Number: 5950507- left
  Part: Headlamp Ring-Outboard
  Usage: 1967-69 Firebird all models; 1965-66 full-size Pontiac (upper headlamp); 1965-72 Tempest, upper outboard headlamp); 1968-74 full-size Pontiac 1970 Grand Prix (left-hand outer lamp).

Interchange Number: 5
  Part Number: 5963209 either side
  Part: Headlamp Ring
  Usage: 1970-73 Firebird all models.

Interchange Number: 6
  Part Number: 5964574 either side
  Part: Headlamp Ring
  Usage: 1974-1976 Firebird all models.

Interchange Number: 7
  Part Number: 9796578 right 9796579 left
  Part: Headlamp Bezel, Inner
  Usage: 1969 Firebird all models.

Interchange Number: 8
  Part Number: 9796576 right 9796577 left
  Part: Headlamp Bezel, Outer
  Usage: 1969 Firebird all models.

Interchange Number: 9
  Part Number: 483412 right 483413 left
  Part: Headlamp Bezel
  Usage: 1970-73 Firebird all models.

Interchange Number: 10
  Part Number: 492666 right 492667 left
  Part: Headlamp Bezel
  Usage: 1974-1976 Firebird all models.

Interchange Number: 11
  Part Number: 5966081 right 5966080 left
  Outer headlamps housings
  Usage: 1977-1981 Firebird all models.

Interchange Number: 12
  Part Number: 5966083 right 5966082 left
  Inner headlamps housings
  Usage: 1977-1981 Firebird all models.

Interchange Number: 13
  Part Number: 5966170 either side
  Headlamp ring fits inner or outer lamps
  Usage: 1977-1981 Firebird all models.

Interchange Number: 14
  Part Number: 10004292 either side
  Bezels fit outer or inner lamps
  Usage: 1979-1981 Firebird except Formula, Trans Am or Esprit
  Notes: Chrome

Interchange Number: 15
  Part Number: 10005236 either side
  Bezels fit outer or inner lamps
  Usage: 1979-1981 Formula, Trans Am or Esprit
  Notes: Black

Standard wiper switch

INTERIOR COMPONENTS

Gauge Assemblies

Trying to tell if a used gauge is functional is nearly impossible in a non-running vehicle, or as a separate part. The most important thing to watch for when buying used gauges is that you get the right cluster. Going from warning lights to a set of fully functional gauges may seem ideal, but there is usually more to the interchange than just slapping in a new instrument cluster. In most cases a new wiring harness from the engine to the instrument cluster will be required to make the gauges function properly.

Next the gauges should be in good condition, no cracked lenses, or broken cases. Check for signs of humidity damage, which will show up as droplets of moisture inside the gauge. Moisture is deadly to electronic equipment, and if you see droplets of water or a fog inside a gauge it is best to reject it. Next check the condition of the face of the gauge and the needle indicator. The numbers or letters should be bright and not faded or worn. The indicator hands should be straight and in working order. Watch out for indicators that are stuck in a non-at rest position. For example: a temperature gauge that is stuck at the hot position, or a speedometer that is resting on the 70-mph mark. This would indicate that it has been damaged, most likely wound too tight, and is unusable. Even though fuel gauges can point to any position and be concerned at normal position, be aware that all salvaged cars must have the gas removed from their tank before going to the yard; it is the law, not to mention much safer. So all fuel gauges should read empty.

1967

Speedometer

Except Rally Cluster

Without Safeguard............................1

With Safeguard..................................3

Rally Cluster

Without Safeguard............................2

With Safe Guard................................4

Tachometer

    Hood Mounted..............................14

    Dash..15

    Ammeter.......................................23

    Oil Pressure..................................25

Fuel Level

Without Rally Cluster..........................31

With Rally Cluster..............................30

Water Temperature............................43

Clock..47

1968

Speedometer

Except Rally Cluster

Without Safeguard............................5

With Safeguard................................6

Rally Cluster

Without Safeguard............................7

With Safe Guard...............................8

Tachometer

  Hood Mounted

  Early..14

  Late...16

  Ammeter..24

  Oil Pressure...................................26

Fuel Gauge

Without Rally Cluster.........................33

With Rally Cluster............................32

Water Temperature............................44

Clock..47

1969

Speedometer

Without Safeguard............................9

With Safeguard................................10

TACHOMETER

Except Rally Cluster..........................17

Rally Cluster..................................18

OIL PRESSURE

Rally Cluster..................................27

Aux. Gauges..................................28

Fuel Level

With Rally, Aux. Gauge Or Safeguard....34

With Rally Cluster............................36

With Aux. Gauges............................37

With Safeguard............................... 35

Water Temperature

Rally Cluster..................................45

Aux. Gauges..................................46

Clock

Rally Cluster..................................48

1970-1971

Speedometer...................................11

Tachometer....................................19

Ammeter.......................................24

Oil Pressure...................................29

Fuel Level

Without Rally Cluster........................ 38

With Rally Cluster............................ 39

With Warning Lamp.......................... 40

Water Temperature........................... 29

Clock

Without Rally Or Aux........................49

With Rally..................................... 50

With Aux Gauge.............................. 51

1972-1975

Speedometer...12

Tachometer..20

Ammeter..24

Oil Pressure..29

Fuel Level

Without Rally Cluster........................ 38

With Rally Cluster.............................. 39

With Warning Lamp......................... 40

Water Temperature.............................29

Clock

Without Rally Or Aux........................ 54

1976-1977

Speedometer
Without Gauges................................59
With Gauges......................................60

Tachometer/Clock.............................56
Water Temperature.............................29
Oil Pressure..29
Fuel Gauge
Without Gauges................................41
With Gauges......................................42
Ammeter..24
Clock
Without Gauges................................54

1978

Speedometer
Without Gauges................................59
With Gauges......................................60
Tachometer/Clock
Early... 53
Late.. 57
Water Temperature.............................29
Oil Pressure.. 29
Fuel Gauge
Without Gauges................................41
With Gauges...................................... 42
Ammeter..24
Clock
Without Gauges................................54

1979

Speedometer
Without Gauges................................59
With Gauges
Except Silver Anniv............................60
Silver Anniversary..............................61
Tachometer 57
Water Temperature
Except Silver Anniv............................64
Silver Anniversary..............................65
Oil Pressure
Except Silver Anniv............................64
Silver Anniversary..............................65
Fuel Gauge
Without Gauges................................41
With Gauges...................................... 42
Ammeter..24
Clock
Without Gauges................................54

1980-1981

Speedometer
Without Gauge................................. 62
With Gauges..................................... 63
Tachometer/Clock.............................58
Water Temperature.............................66
Oil Pressure..66
Fuel Gauge
Without Gauges................................68
With Gauges......................................69
Ammeter..70
Clock
Without Gauges................................71

Interchange Number: 1
Part Number: 6480794
Part: Speedometer
Usage: 1967 Firebird, except with Safeguard or Rally cluster.

Interchange Number: 2
Part Number: 6481283
Part: Speedometer
Usage: 1967 Firebird, with Rally cluster. Except Safe guard

Interchange Number: 3
Part Number: 6480796
Part: Speedometer
Usage: 1967 Firebird, except with Safeguard except Rally cluster.

Interchange Number: 4
   Part Number: 6481254
   Part: Speedometer
   Usage: 1967 Firebird, with Safeguard and Rally cluster.

Interchange Number: 5
   Part Number: 6481931
   Part: Speedometer
   Usage: 1968 Firebird, except with Safeguard or Rally cluster.

Interchange Number: 6
   Part Number: 6481932
   Part: Speedometer
   Usage: 1968 Firebird, with Safeguard except Rally cluster.

Interchange Number: 7
   Part Number: 6481933
   Part: Speedometer
   Usage: 1968 Firebird, with Rally cluster. Except Safeguard.

Interchange Number: 8
   Part Number: 6481934
   Part: Speedometer
   Usage: 1968 Firebird, with Safeguard and Rally cluster.

Interchange Number: 9
   Part Number: 6492260
   Part: Speedometer
   Usage: 1969 Firebird, without Safeguard.

Interchange Number: 10
   Part Number: 6492261
   Part: Speedometer
   Usage: 1969 Firebird, with Safeguard.

Interchange Number: 11
   Part Number: 6492882
   Part: Speedometer
   Usage: 1970-71 Firebird; 1972 Firebird without seat belt warning.

Interchange Number: 12
   Part Number: 6497947
   Part: Speedometer
   Usage: 1972-74 Firebird with seat belt warning.

Interchange Number: 13
   Part Number: 8986779
   Part: Speedometer
   Usage: 1975 Firebird.

Interchange Number: 14
   Part Number: 6468670
   Part: Tachometer
   Usage: 1967-early 1968 Firebird
   Notes: 6,500 rpm redline

Interchange Number: 15
   Part Number: 6468675
   Part: Tachometer
   Usage: 1967 Firebird

Interchange Number: 16
   Part Number: 6468956
   Part: Tachometer
   Usage: Late 1968 Firebird; 1968 Tempest.
   Notes: Hood mount 5,500 rpm redline

Interchange Number: 17
   Part Number: 6469424
   Part: Tachometer
   Usage: 1969 Firebird, except Rally cluster
   Notes: Instrument panel mount.

Interchange Number: 18
   Part Number: 6469499
   Part: Tachometer
   Usage: 1969 Firebird, with Rally cluster
   Notes: Instrument panel mount.

Interchange Number: 19
   Part Number: 6469962
   Part: Tachometer
   Usage: 1970-71 Firebird. All with aux. Gauge package.

Example of Rally gauges

Interchange Number: 20
Part Number: Part:
Tachometer
Usage: 1972-74 Firebird, with Rally cluster
Notes: Instrument panel mount.

Interchange Number: 21
Part Number: Part:
Tachometer
Usage: 1975 Firebird, with Rally cluster
Notes: Instrument panel mount.

Interchange Number: 22
Part Number: 6473156
Part: Ammeter
Usage: 1967 Firebird, all models.

Interchange Number: 23
Part Number: 6473250
Part: Ammeter
Usage: 1968 Firebird, all models.

Interchange Number: 24
Part Number: 6473740
Part: Ammeter
Usage: 1970-1979 Firebird, with aux. gauge package; 1977-1979 full size Pontiac with gauges.

Interchange Number: 25
Part Number: 6461289
Part: Oil Pressure
Usage: 1967 Firebird, with Rally gauge package.

Interchange Number: 26
Part Number: 6461552
Part: Oil Pressure
Usage: 1968 Firebird, with Rally gauge package.

Interchange Number: 27
Part Number: 6461987
Part: Oil Pressure
Usage: 1969 Firebird, Tempest, Grand Prix with Rally gauge package.

Interchange Number: 28
Part Number: 6462170
Part: Oil Pressure
Usage: 1969 Firebird, with aux. gauge package.

Interchange Number: 29
Part Number: 6493193
Part: Oil Pressure and Water Temp.
Usage: 1970-1978 Firebird, with Rally gauge package and clock.

Interchange Number: 30
Part Number: 6430659
Part: Fuel Gauge
Usage: 1967 Firebird, with Rally gauge package.

Interchange Number: 31
Part Number: 6480802
Part: Fuel Gauge
Usage: 1967 Firebird, without Rally gauge package.

Interchange Number: 32
Part Number: 64309030
Part: Fuel Gauge
Usage: 1968 Firebird, with Rally gauge package.

Interchange Number: 33
Part Number: 6431007
Part: Fuel Gauge
Usage: 1968 Firebird, without Rally gauge package.

Interchange Number: 34
Part Number: 6431093
Part: Fuel Gauge
Usage: 1969 Firebird, Tempest, Grand Prix without Rally gauge package, Safeguard or export.

Interchange Number: 35
Part Number: 6431094
Part: Fuel Gauge
Usage: 1969 Firebird, Tempest, Grand Prix with Safeguard.

Interchange Number: 36
 Part Number: 6431155
 Part: Fuel Gauge
 Usage: 1969 Firebird, Tempest, Grand Prix with Rally gauge package.

Interchange Number: 37
 Part Number: 6431173
 Part: Fuel Gauge
 Usage: 1969 Firebird, with aux. gauge package.

Interchange Number: 38
 Part Number: 6431309
 Part: Fuel Gauge
 Usage: 1970-74 Firebird, without aux. gauge package, or warning lamp.

Interchange Number: 39
 Part Number: 6431428
 Part: Fuel Gauge
 Usage: 1970-74 Firebird, with aux. gauge package.

Interchange Number: 40
 Part Number: 6431393
 Part: Fuel Gauge
 Usage: 1970-74 Firebird, with warning lamp.

Interchange Number: 41
 Part Number: 6432003
 Part: Fuel Gauge
 Usage: 1975-1979 Firebird, 1975-1977 LeMans, LeMans Sport, Grand LeMans: without Rally gauge package or economy fuel gauge.

Interchange Number: 42
 Part Number: 6432039
 Part: Fuel Gauge
 Usage: 1975-1979 Firebird, with Rally gauge package.

Interchange Number: 43
 Part Number: 6402854
 Part: Water Temperature
 Usage: 1967 Firebird, with aux. gauge package.

Interchange Number: 44
 Part Number: 6488826
 Part: Water Temperature
 Usage: 1968 Firebird, with Rally gauge package.

Interchange Number: 45
 Part Number: 6489331
 Part: Water Temperature
 Usage: 1969 Firebird, with Rally gauge package.

Interchange Number: 46
 Part Number: 6489469
 Part: Water Temperature
 Usage: 1969 Firebird, with aux. gauge package.

Interchange Number: 47
 Part Number: 9793259
 Part: Clock
 Usage: 1967-68 Firebird, with aux. gauge package. Floor mount.

Interchange Number: 48
 Part Number: 9796899
 Part: Clock
 Usage: 1969 Firebird, with clock.

Interchange Number: 49
 Part Number: 480614
 Part: Clock
 Usage: 1970-72 Firebird, without Rally gauge package.

Interchange Number: 50
 Part Number: 480739
 Part: Clock
 Usage: 1970-72 Firebird, with Rally gauge package.
 Notes: Interchange number 52 will fit, and was replacement part.

Interchange Number: 51
 Part Number: 6470000
 Part: Clock
 Usage: 1970-72 Firebird, with aux. gauge package.

Interchange Number: 52
 Part Number: 492874
 Part: Clock
 Usage: 1973-75 Firebird, with Rally gauge package.

Interchange Number: 53
 Part Number: 5658246
 Part: Clock/Tachometer
 Usage: 1973-early 1978 Firebird, with Rally gauge package or fuel economy gauge.

Interchange Number: 54
 Part Number: 492869
 Part: Clock
 Usage: 1974-1979 Firebird, 1974-1977 LeMans, Grand Prix, all models and body styles without Rally gauge package.

Interchange Number: 55
 Part Number: 6464223
 Part: Vacuum Gauge
 Usage: 1975 Firebird with fuel economy gauge.

Interchange Number: 56
Part Number: 5659065
Part: Tachometer
Usage: 1976-early 1978 Firebird, with Rally gauge package.
Notes: Has fixed hub.

Interchange Number: 57
Part Number: 5659391
Part: Tachometer
Usage: late 1978-1979 Firebird, with Rally gauge package
Notes: Has tach pointer that rotates.

Interchange Number: 58
Part Number: 5659837
Part: Tachometer/clock
Usage 1980-1981 Firebird, with Rally gauge package

Interchange Number: 59
Part Number: 25024034
Part: Speedometer
Usage: 1976-1979 Firebird, without gauge.

Interchange Number: 60
Part Number: 25024035
Part: Speedometer
Usage: 1976-1979 Firebird, with gauges. Except with Y89

Interchange Number: 61
Part Number: 25024038
Part: Speedometer
Usage: 1979 silver Anniversary Trans Am

Interchange Number: 62
Part Number: 25022022
Part: Speedometer
Usage: 1980 Firebird without gauge; 1981 Firebird without gauges except export.

Interchange Number: 63
Part Number: 25022023
Part: Speedometer
Usage: 1980 Firebird with gauge

Interchange Number: 64
Part Number:
Part: Water Temp/Oil Pressure
Usage: 1979 Firebird with gauges except Silver Anniversary

Interchange Number: 65
Part Number: 8993714
Part Water Temp/Oil Pressure
Usage: 1979 Silver Anniversary Trans Am

Interchange Number: 66
Part Number: 8993699
Part: water temp.
Usage: 1980-1981 Firebird with gauges

Interchange Number: 67
Part Number: 8993338
Part: Oil Pressure and temp
Usage: 1979 Firebird with gauges except Silver Anniversary

Interchange Number: 68
Part Number: 6432891
Part: Fuel Gauge
Usage: 1980-1981 Firebird without gauge

Interchange Number: 69
Part Number: 6432975
Part: Fuel Gauge
Usage: 1980-1981 Firebird with gauges

Interchange Number: 70
Part Number: 6474616
Part: Amp. Meter
Usage: 1980-1981 Firebird with gauges

Interchange Number: 71
Part Number: 25022343
Part: Clock
Usage: 1980-1981 Firebird without gauges

1967 instrumentation

1967 Standard Speedometer

1967 Speedometer with gauges.

Standard 1967 fuel gauge

1967 gauges.

1967 hood mounted tachometer

1969 Speedometer without gauges

1969 Standard fuel gauges

1969 Clock

1970-1971 speedometer

1970-1971 Tachometer

1970-1978 Water temp and oil pressure gauges

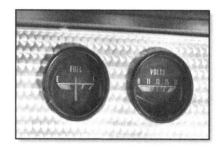

1970-1975 Fuel and 1970-1978 ammeter

1970-1971 Standard warning lights

1970-1971 standard fuel gauge.

1976-1979 standard warning lights

1972-1975 Speedometer was used with or Without gauges

1972-1975 Tachometer

1976-1977 Tachometer

1976-1979 Speedometer with gauges, except 1979 Silver Anniversary

1976-1979 standard speedometer

Early 1978 Tachometer

1977-1978 gas gauge with gauges.

1980-1981 Speedometer with gauges

1980-1981 Tachometer

Dome Lamp

1967-1968

Base...1

Lens..3

1969-1975

Base...2

Lens..4

1976-1981

Base...5

Lens..6

Interchange Number: 1
   Part Number: 4866918
   Part: Base (Reflector)
   Usage: 1967-68 Firebird, hardtop models only.

Interchange Number: 2
   Part Number: 8732779
   Part: Base (Reflector) with rim
   Usage: 1969-1975 Firebird, hardtop models only; 1969-75 Tempest, full-size Pontiac, Grand Prix, all body styles except convertible; 1969-1975 Cutlass, Chevelle, Skylark all body styles except convertible

Interchange Number: 3
   Part Number: 6279669
   Part: Lens
   Usage: 1967-68 Firebird, hardtop models only.

Interchange Number: 4
   Part Number: 8732777
   Part: Lens
   Usage: 1969-1975 Firebird, hardtop models only; 1969-75 Tempest, full-size Pontiac, Grand Prix, all body styles except convertible; 1969-1975 Cutlass, Chevelle, Skylark all body styles except convertible.

Interchange Number: 5
   Part Number: 1695635
   Part: Base
   Usage: 1976-1981 Firebird, LeMans, full-size Pontiac 1976-1977 Grand Prix; 1976-1977 Cutlass, Chevelle, Skylark; 1980-1981 Phoenix except hatchback

Interchange Number: 6
   Part Number: 1695626
   Part: Lens
   Usage: 1976-1981 Firebird, LeMans, full-size Pontiac 1976-1977 Grand Prix; 1976-1977 Cutlass, Chevelle, Skylark;

Turn Signal, Lever

1967

Without Cruise Control.....................1

With Cruise Control..........................3

1968-1975

Without Cruise Control.....................2

With Cruise Control..........................3

Interchange Number: 1
   Part Number: 3909580
   Usage: 1967 Firebird, without cruise control.

Interchange Number: 2
   Part Number: 9786981
   Usage: 1968-1978 Firebird without cruise control; 1968-1972 Tempest, all models except with cruise control; 1973-1977 LeMans, LeMans Sport, Grand LeMans, full-size Pontiac, except with cruise control.

Interchange Number: 3
   Part Number: 6465256
   Usage: 1967-1978 Firebird, 1967-1977 Lemans 1967-1976, full-size Pontiac with cruise control; 1976-1981 Phoenix with speed control

Interchange Number: 4
   Part Number: 546777
   Usage: 1978-1981 Firebird, 1977-1981 full-size Pontiac; 1978-1981 Lemans, Grand Prix without cruise control

Interchange Number: 5
   Part Number: 25030492
   Usage: 1978-1981 Firebird, 1977-1981 full-size Pontiac; 1978-1981 Lemans, Grand Prix with cruise control

Heater, Air Conditioning Controls

1967
Without Air Conditioning..................1
With Air Conditioning......................2

1968
Without Air Conditioning................. 1
With Air Conditioning...................... 3

1969
Without Air Conditioning.................. 4
With Air Conditioning...................... 5

1970
EXCEPT TRANS AM

Without Air Conditioning.................. 13
With Air Conditioning...................... 14

TRANS AM

Without Air conditioning.................. 11
With Air Conditioning...................... 12

1971-1972
EXCEPT TRANS AM

Without Air Conditioning.................. 15
With Air Conditioning...................... 16

TRANS AM

Without Air Conditioning.................. 11
With Air Conditioning...................... 12

1973
EXCEPT TRANS AM

Without Air Conditioning.................. 15
With Air Conditioning...................... 16

TRANS AM

Without Air Conditioning.................. 7
With Air Conditioning...................... 12

1974-1976
EXCEPT TRANS AM

Without Air Conditioning.................. 15
With Air Conditioning...................... 9

TRANS AM

Without Air Conditioning.................. 7
With Air Conditioning...................... 10

1976
EXCEPT TRANS AM

Without Air Conditioning
Early.. 15
Late... 17

With Air Conditioning...................... 9

TRANS AM

Without Air Conditioning
Early.. 7
Late... 17

With Air Conditioning......................10

1977-1978
Without Air Conditioning..................17
With Air Conditioning......................18

1979
Without Air Conditioning...................17

With Air Conditioning
Except Silver Anniversary 18
Silver Anniversary............................19

1980-1981
Without Air Conditioning...................17
With Air Conditioning......................18

Interchange Number: 1
  Part Number: 7303092
  Usage: 1967-68 Firebird, without air conditioning.

Interchange Number: 2
  Part Number: 3891797
  Usage: 1967 Firebird, with air conditioning.

Interchange Number: 3
  Part Number: 7303112
  Usage: 1968 Firebird, without air conditioning.

Interchange Number: 4
  Part Number: 7307802
  Usage: 1969 Firebird, tempest, all models except air conditioning.

Interchange Number: 5
  Part Number: 7307832
  Usage: 1969 Firebird, with air conditioning.

Interchange Number: 6
  Part Number: 7307832
  Usage: 1969 Firebird, without air conditioning.

Interchange Number: 7
  Part Number: 7938582
  Usage: 1973- early 1976 Trans Am without air conditioning.
  Notes: Marked De-ice.

Interchange Number: 8
  Part Number: 7938582
  Usage: 1972- early 1976 Trans Am without air conditioning.

Interchange Number: 9
  Part Number: 9349732
  Usage: 1974- 1976 Firebird, with air conditioning, except

Interchange Number: 10
  Part Number: 934946502
  Usage: 1974-1976 Trans Am with air conditioning.

Interchange Number: 11
  Part Number: 7930582
  Usage: 1970-72 Trans Am without air conditioning.

Interchange Number: 12
  Part Number: 7930592
  Usage: 1970-71 Trans Am with air conditioning.

Interchange Number: 13
  Part Number: 7312272
  Usage: 1970 Firebird without air conditioning, except Trans Am.

Interchange Number: 14
  Part Number: 7312182
  Usage: 1970 Firebird with air conditioning, except Trans Am

Interchange Number: 15
  Part Number: 7935372
  Usage: 1971-72 Firebird without air conditioning, except Trans Am.

Interchange Number: 16
  Part Number: 79353482
  Usage: 1971-72 Firebird with air conditioning, except Trans Am.

Interchange Number: 17
  Part Number: 16004442
  Usage: Late 1976 Firebird without air conditioning,

Interchange Number: 18
  Part Number: 16011632
  Usage: 1977-1981 Firebird with air conditioning, except Silver Anniversary

Interchange Number: 19
  Part Number: 16011682
  Usage: 1979 Trans Am Silver Anniversary; 1980-1981 Special Edition Trans Am with Air conditioning

Heater Components
1967-1968

MOTOR

Without Air Conditioning.................. 1

With Air Conditioning...................... 2

CORE

Without Air Conditioning................. 3

With Air Conditioning...................... 4

1969-1976

MOTOR

Without Air Conditioning....................1

With Air Conditioning....................... 2

CORE

Without Air Conditioning................... 5

With Air Conditioning...................... 6

1977

MOTOR

Without Air Conditioning....................1

With Air Conditioning
Early... 2
Late.. 7

CORE

Without Air Conditioning.................. 5

With Air Conditioning...................... 6

1978-1981

MOTOR

Without Air Conditioning....................1

With Air Conditioning....................... 7

CORE

Without Air Conditioning.................. 5

With Air Conditioning...................... 6

Interchange Number: 1
Part Number: 5044555
Usage: 1967-1981 Firebird, Camaro; 1964-1981 Lemans, Chevelle, Cutlass, Skylark; 1963-75 full-size Pontiac, full-size Chevrolet, full-size Buick; 1964-81 full-size Oldsmobile; 1973-79 Apollo; 1971-79 Ventura II; 1968-75 Toronado; 1971-75 Vega; 1969-77 Grand Prix; 1971-76 Cadillac; 1973-79 Omega; 1967-79 Nova. All models listed are without air conditioning.

Interchange Number: 2
Part Number: 5044559
Usage: 1967-early 1977 Firebird, Camaro; 1964-77 Lemans, Chevelle, Cutlass, Skylark; 1963-77 full-size Pontiac, full-size Chevrolet, full-size Buick; 1964-77 full-size Oldsmobile; 1973-77 Apollo; 1971-77 Ventura II; 1968-75 Toronado; 1971-75 Vega; 1969-77 Grand Prix; 1971-75 Cadillac; 1973-77 Omega; 1967-77 Nova. All models listed are with air conditioning.

Interchange Number: 3
Part Number: 3022074
Usage: 1967-68 Firebird, without air conditioning; 1968 Camaro, without air conditioning.

Interchange Number: 4
Part Number: 3022068
Usage: 1967-68 Firebird, Camaro with air conditioning.

Interchange Number: 5
Part Number: 3016842
Usage: 1969-81 Firebird, 1969-81 Camaro, except 396-ci; 1968-79 Nova; 1973-749Apollo, Omega; 1971-75 Ventura II. All models listed are without air conditioning.

Interchange Number: 6
Part Number: 3016842
Usage: 1969-81 Firebird, 1969-81 Camaro, except 396-ci; 1968-79 Nova; 1973-79 Apollo, Omega; 1971-75 Ventura II. All models listed are with air conditioning.

Interchange Number: 7
Part Number: 2202945
Usage: Late 1977-1981 Firebird, Camaro; 1978-82 Lemans, Chevelle, Cutlass, Skylark; 1978-1983 full-size Pontiac, full-size Chevrolet, full-size Buick; 1978-83 full-size Oldsmobile; 1978-83 Monte Carlo, Grand Prix All with air conditioning.

Wiper Motor

1967

All... 1

1968

All... 2

1969

All... 2

1970-1972

Except Recessed............................. 2

Recessed (Hidden),..........................3

1973

Except Recessed............................. 2

Recessed (Hidden)

Early.. 3

Late... 4

1974-1977

Except Recessed............................. 2

Recessed (Hidden)......................... 4

1978-1981

Without Pulse wiper....................... 5

With Pulse Wiper............................ 6

Interchange Number: 1
> Part Number: 491476
> Usage: 1967 Firebird, Camaro; 1964-67 Tempest, Chevelle, Cutlass, Skylark; 1963-69 Corvair. All models have two-speed wiper.

Interchange Number: 2
> Part Number: 4918442
> Usage: 1968-77 Firebird, Camaro; 1968-77 Tempests, Chevelle, Cutlass, Skylark, Nova; 1971-77 Ventura II; 1974 Apollo, Omega. All models are without recess (hidden) wipers.

Interchange Number: 3
> Part Number: 4939586
> Usage: 1970-early 1973 Firebird, Camaro; 1968-72 Tempest, Chevelle, Skylark, Cutlass, all models Listed are with recess (hidden) wipers.

Interchange Number: 4
> Part Number: 4960951
> Usage: Late 1973-1977 Firebird, Camaro; with recess (hidden) wipers.

Interchange Number: 5
> Part Number: 4960951
> Usage: Late 1973-1981 Firebird, Camaro; with recess (hidden) wipers without pulse wipers.

Interchange Number: 6
> Part Number: 22009215
> Usage: 1978-1981 Firebird, Camaro; with pulse wipers.

Wiper Washer Jar

1967-1969

All... 1

1970-1972

All... 2

1973-1974

All... 3

1975-1977

All... 4

1978-1981

All... 5

Interchange Number: 1
   Part Number: 3840083
   Usage: 1967-69 Firebird; 1962-66 full-size Pontiac; 1964-66 Tempest; 1964-67 Cutlass

Interchange Number: 2
   Part Number: 3961557
   Usage: 1970-72 Firebird; 1971-72 Tempest, Grand Prix, all models and body styles; 1971-72 Ventura II.
   Notes: Interchange number 3 will fit

Interchange Number: 3
   Part Number: 3990892
   Usage: 1973-74 Firebird, Ventura II; 1970 Camaro, full-size Chevrolet; 1971-74 Nova,; 1970-72 Chevelle; 1973-74 Omega

Interchange Number: 4
   Part Number: 4999857
   Usage: 1975-1977 Firebird

Interchange Number: 5
   Part Number: 461252
   Usage: 1978-1981 Firebird

Wiper Switch

1967-1968

All..8

1969

All..7

1970-1972

Without recess wipers...........................5
With recess wipers................................6

1973-1977

Without recess wipers...........................1
With recess wipers................................2

1978-1979

Without pulse wiper.............................2
With Pulse wipers................................3

1980-1981

Without pulse wiper.............................2
With Pulse wipers................................4

Interchange Number: 1
   Part Number: 1994178
   Usage: 1973-1977 Firebird without recess wipers.

Interchange Number: 2
   Part Number: 199417
   Usage: 1973-1981 Firebird, full-size 1973-1977 Pontiac with recess wipers except pulse wiper

Interchange Number: 3
   Part Number: 497234
   Usage: 1978-1979 Firebird with pulse wiper

Interchange Number: 4
   Part Number: 10010666
   Usage: 1980-1981 Firebird with pulse wiper

Interchange Number: 5
   Part Number: 1994090
   Usage: 1970-1972 Firebird without recess wipers

Interchange Number: 6
   Part Number: 1994089
   Usage: 1970-1972 Firebird with recess wipers

Interchange Number: 7
   Part Number: 1993453
   Usage: 1969 Firebird

Interchange Number: 8
   Part Number: 1993684
   Usage: 1967-1968 Firebird, Camaro

Headlamp Switch

1967

All..1

1968-1977

All..2

1978-1981

All..3

Interchange Number: 1
   Part Number: 1995179
   Usage: 1967 Firebird, Camaro; 1964-1967 Tempest.

Interchange Number: 2
   Part Number: 1995199
   Usage: 1968-1977 Firebird,

Interchange Number: 3
   Part Number: 1995217
   Usage: 1978-1981 Firebird, full-size Pontiac, Phoenix,Sunbird
   Notes: Knob differs between models swap without knob.

Entry	Page
Air Extractors	19
Ammeter	102
Arm Rest, Front	87
Back Glass	50
Body Numbers	6
Clock	103
Console	88
Convertible Lifts	45
Crash Pad	82
Door Handle, Inside	30
Door Handle, Outside	29
Door Hinge	29
Door Lock	33
Door Panels	86
Door Shells	28
Door, Glovebox	75
Emblems, Bumper	53
Emblems, Front Fender	59
Emblems, Front Header	53
Emblems, Grille	53
Emblems, Hood	56
Emblems, Rear Panel	62
Engine VIN Codes	7
Fender, Skirts	18
Fenders	17
Fisher Body Tag	9
Front Bumper	26
Front End Panel	26
Front Fenders	17
Fuel Gauge	103
Gauge Assemblies	101
Glove Box	75
Grilles	21
Headlamp Bezels	100
Headlamp Rings	100
Headlamp Switch	113
Heater, Air Conditioning Controls	109
Heater, Core	110
Heater, Motor	110
Hinges, Hood	16
Hood	13
Hood Latch	17
Hood Springs	16
Housings, Headlamps	100
Instrument Panel,	72
Interior Trim Codes	10
Lamp, Dome	108
Lamps, Front Turn	92
Lamps, license plate	97
Lamps, Side, Front	94
Louvers	19
Markers, Side Rear	94
Mirror, Inside	76
Mirror, Outside	34
Mirrors	28
Nameplates	52
Nameplates, Instrument Panel	83
Oil Pressure	103
Panel, Rear Tail Lamp	40
Panel, Vent Duct	74
Quarter Glass	50
Quarter Panels, Inside	86
Rear Bumper	40
Rear Fender Flares	42
Rear Quarter Panels	37
Rear Shelf Panel	90
Rear Spoilers	42
Removing Grilles	21
Rocker Panels	45
Roof Panels	44
Seat Adjustment Rails	79
Seat Belts	91
Seat Frames	77
Shoulder Straps	91
Speedometer	101
Spoiler, Front	27
Tachometer	102
Tail Lamps	94
Trim And Nameplates, Door Panel	87
Trim, Doors	67
Trim, Front Extension	69
Trim, Front Fenders	67
Trim, Hood	65
Trim, Radio Panel Cover	85
Trim, Rear Quarter Panel	69
Trim, Rear Quarters	69
Trim, Rear Window	71
Trim, Rocker Panel	68
Trim, Roof Drip Rails	68
Trim, Windshield	65
Trunk Floor	39
Trunk Lid, Hinges	38
Trunk Lids	38
Trunk Lock	39
Turn Signal, Lever	108
Uni-Body	46
Vehicle Identification Number	6
Vent Glass	49
Window Regulator	32
Window Regulator Handle	31
Windshield	48
Wiper Motor	112
Wiper Switch	113
Wiper Washer Jar	112

Made in the USA
Columbia, SC
02 October 2022